Red Ha... ...d Engineer (RHCE) Study Guide

Ansible Automation for the Red Hat Enterprise Linux 8 Exam (EX294)

Andrew Mallett

Apress®

Red Hat Certified Engineer (RHCE) Study Guide

Andrew Mallett
Peterborough, UK

ISBN-13 (pbk): 978-1-4842-6860-5   ISBN-13 (electronic): 978-1-4842-6861-2
https://doi.org/10.1007/978-1-4842-6861-2

Managing Director, Apress Media LLC: Welmoed Spahr
Acquisitions Editor: Divya Modi
Development Editor: Laura Berendson
Coordinating Editor: Divya Modi

Cover designed by eStudioCalamar

Cover image designed by Pixabay

Distributed to the book trade worldwide by Springer Science+Business Media New York, 1 New York Plaza, Suite 4600, New York, NY 10004-1562, USA. Phone 1-800-SPRINGER, fax (201) 348-4505, e-mail orders-ny@springer-sbm.com, or visit www.springeronline.com. Apress Media, LLC is a California LLC and the sole member (owner) is Springer Science + Business Media Finance Inc (SSBM Finance Inc). SSBM Finance Inc is a **Delaware** corporation.

For information on translations, please e-mail booktranslations@springernature.com; for reprint, paperback, or audio rights, please e-mail bookpermissions@springernature.com.

Apress titles may be purchased in bulk for academic, corporate, or promotional use. eBook versions and licenses are also available for most titles. For more information, reference our Print and eBook Bulk Sales web page at www.apress.com/bulk-sales.

Any source code or other supplementary material referenced by the author in this book is available to readers on GitHub via the book's product page, located at www.apress.com/ 978-1-4842-6860-5. For more detailed information, please visit www.apress.com/source-code.

Printed on acid-free paper

To Joan, my always present wife and friend.

Table of Contents

About the Author

Andrew Mallett is a well-known Linux consultant and trainer; his YouTube Channel has over 65K subscribers and more than 1,000 videos. Working mainly online now, he has authored courses on both Pluralsight and Udemy, and regularly teaches classes online to a worldwide audience. Andrew is familiar with Linux and UNIX and has worked with them for over 20 years. Scripting and automation are one of his passions, as he is inherently lazy and will always seek the most effective way of getting the job done. The Urban Penguin, his alter ego, is a UK-based company where he creates his work and currently employs five people.

About the Technical Reviewer

Himanshu Tank, Currently works as a Technical Consultant and serving Airtel as a Cloud Engineer. He is a Red Hat Certified Architect in Infrastructures (RHCA), and a Red Hat Certified Engineer (RHCE). He applies his knowledge in the fields of DevOps, Cloud, and on core products by Red Hat such as Ansible, OpenShift, OpenStack, CEPH Storage, Linux Troubleshooting and Diagnostics, and Server Security and Hardening.

Introduction

For many years the RHCE from Red Hat has been based on managing services on a single Red Hat host. The big question is: *how many RHCEs manage just a single host?* With that in mind, Red Hat has updated the exam and training to support Ansible, allowing you to learn to manage many hosts.

Ansible is a configuration management system that is now owned by Red Hat Inc. Using Ansible, you can manage many systems as easily as you can manage a single system. Using this book, *Red Hat Certified Engineer (RHCE) Study Guide: Ansible Automation for the Red Hat Enterprise Linux 8 Exam (EX294)*, you will be able to start without previous knowledge of Ansible. We take you from zero knowledge to be being exam ready with the 15 well-written chapters, each with practical examples that you can implement in your own environment.

We emphasize the need for practical examples, allowing you to really learn Ansible and learn it well. Although the exam will focus solely on Red Hat Enterprise Linux 8, we use both CentOS 8 and Ubuntu 18.04, permitting you to see some really cool features of Ansible that allow easy integration with multiple Linux distributions. I really do believe that this book offers better Ansible training than a course or training based on a single Linux distribution.

By the end of this book you will be ready for the exam, because you have been able to invest time in practicing the examples shown throughout the book. This will include installing Ansible on both CentOS and Ubuntu, and configuring the host inventory and Ansible configuration. You will begin your familiarity of Ansible by using ad hoc commands directly from the command line. Using ad hoc commands, you do not need to create

Playbooks and you can get straight into configuring our remote managed devices. These commands introduce Ansible modules, and you will learn how to use examples straight from the documentation.

You will soon learn that ad hoc commands are an awesome quick start, but we need Playbooks to create repeatably correct configurations that are documented. Yes, the configuration files also act as your documentation showing how the hosts should be configured. You will learn to write YAML, the language used in Playbooks, as well as learning to configure your text editor to be an effective YAML editor.

Your main project that you work with during the book allows you to deploy an Apache-based LAMP server on both CentOS and Ubuntu. You will deploy web content that includes static web pages as well as PHP pages to see your stack in action. In deploying LAMP with Ansible, you will learn to use roles, tasks, handlers, variables, and conditional statements—all of which are required in the exam and in your workplace.

As an experienced Ansible administrator and trainer, I am able to help you prepare for the exam and share some of my knowledge, and I am honored to be on this journey with you.

CHAPTER 1

Understanding Ansible and the Red Hat RHCE

Red Hat has always led the way with their enterprise Linux solutions and the certification programs that followed. For Linux administrators the pinnacle of certification has always been the RHCE, the Red Hat Certified Engineer. With the purchase of Ansible by Red Hat, they again lead the way by making configuration management the focus of your administrative efforts and the new RHCE. Enterprises have to make money and become more efficient; by using configuration management systems such as Ansible, one administrator can now do the same job as ten administrators. It is important that you become that one in ten, and you learn and certify in Ansible.

Note The word "ansible" was first used by the author Ursula K. Le Guin in her 1966 novel Rocannon's World. As a contraction of the word "answerable," it references fictional devices that can send messages over interstellar distances to managed systems. Ansible from Red Hat may not work over interstellar distances, but it certainly does manage devices usually located on planet Earth.

© Andrew Mallett 2021
A. Mallett, *Red Hat Certified Engineer (RHCE) Study Guide*,
https://doi.org/10.1007/978-1-4842-6861-2_1

In this first chapter, I start you on your RHCE journey with Ansible and introduce you to the Red Hat certifications and to the Ansible product. It would be both amazing and an honor for me if you want to follow along with your own lab systems, allowing you to gain that all important practice. Understanding that need, I will explain the systems that I use throughout the book and what you will need as a minimum to complete your own practices. You certainly can use this book as a study guide but also, and more importantly, you can use this book to learn Ansible. The information that I give you here is geared for real life as well as for the exam. The exam will, understandably, focus solely on Red Hat Enterprise Linux for your managed devices. Making use of other Linux distributions, I use Ubuntu systems as well, allowing you to harness the real power of Ansible even if we don't reach interstellar distances.

Red Hat and Ansible

The Red Hat corporation, based in Raleigh NC, purchased Ansible in 2015. Originally written by Michael DeHaan, Ansible is an agentless configuration management system that can be used to manage Linux, Unix, Microsoft Windows, and managed network systems. Managing your estate from the Ansible controller, the system with Ansible installed, means that you can manage more systems and more easily. Ansible both documents and enforces the configuration and is perfect to ensure that you meet both enterprise and compliance requirements. In a world of uncertainty, having the agility to quickly deploy systems in the dictated configuration reliably every time is an absolute gift. Ansible is free and open source; there is no cost in deploying Ansible to manage your systems and assist in your efficiency.

Other configuration management systems based in Linux include:

- Puppet from PuppetLabs

- Chef from chef.io

- Salt from SaltStack

Red Hat Certifications

As I mentioned earlier, Red Hat is at the forefront in Linux certifications, having the most desirable credibility and recognition. Taking the exam will test your knowledge in a practical way, providing you with live systems to configure into the desired state. Certification begins with the RHCSA; with that taken and passed you can then sit the RHCE.

RHCSA

The start of your Red Hat certification journey is the Red Hat Certified System Administrator, commonly known as the RHCSA. Testing you in your Linux administration skills, currently in Red Hat Enterprise Linux 8, you can prove to yourself and the world that you are among the best. You will need to demonstrate management of the file system, users, permissions, networking, and others. You can gain these skills through nine days of classroom training based on a five-day course, RH124, followed by a four-day course, RH134. With this learning under your belt, you will be accomplished and most deserved in proving your skills with the exam.

RHCE

The latest version of the Red Hat Certified Engineer, launched in 2019, sees potential candidates, having already certified as an RHCSA, pitting their skills in a contest with Ansible and Red Hat Enterprise Linux 8. They do so by configuring the target systems in the desired state laid out by the exam developers. Your task is made simpler, as you will have gained the requisite skills from this book or the classroom training of four days with the RH294 course. Using Ansible, you can quickly configure managed devices into the desired state, usually from YAML files known as *Playbooks* or, occasionally, ad hoc commands executed at the command line of the Ansible controller.

Lab Systems

Throughout this book we will use CentOS 8, a free rebuild of Red Hat Enterprise Linux. In the exam you will be expected to use Red Hat, but CentOS and Red Hat are directly comparable. As well as this Red Hat-based distribution, we will use a Debian-based distribution, Ubuntu 18.04. This allows you to learn more about Ansible and how we can easily integrate multiple distributions into our Ansible management. Ansible and most configuration management systems are *agnostic* of the underlying OS. We ask for the configuration to be made without any care on how that is achieved. Making use of system variables, or facts, we can determine the OS from the *os_family* fact and modify any action to meet the needs of the target OS, such as differing package or service names. Your learning of Ansible will be enhanced if you can use multiple distributions, but if you are limited in the system available to you, you must have at least one CentOS 8 system.

Note   We use two CentOS 8 systems and one Ubuntu 18.04 system.

These systems can take any form; you just need to have full administrative access to them. These can be physical systems, virtual systems that you host, or hosted within the cloud. As this book will be developed over a few months, I will use internal virtual machines hosted in VMware Fusion in MacOS rather than the cloud. Using cloud-based systems can be a great idea if you can get your studies complete in a few weeks. The reality is, the virtualization engine used in not relevant to Ansible. You will need to use CentOS 8 as your Ansible controller; it's the only system needing software added to it, as Ansible does not require agents on the managed devices. Each device that you will manage from the controller will need to be accessible to the controller over the network on TCP port 22, SSH. Ideally, your lab environment would have the managed devices hosted on the same network, but this is not a requirement.

On each of my lab systems I will always create an account named *tux*; this account should be added to the administrator`s group in the distribution. This is the *wheel* group in CentOS and the *sudo* group in Ubuntu.

Installing Ansible on CentOS 8

You will be expected to work with Red Hat Enterprise Linux 8 in the exam; here we use the rebuild of this (i.e., CentOS 8). We only need to install Ansible on this one system, CentOS 8. The Ubuntu systems do not need additional software installed. This system becomes our Ansible controller and could quite feasibly be your Linux workstation in the enterprise. We will use a CentOS 8 server without a GUI installed. If you are starting a clean install for the labs, a minimal installation of the CentOS 8 server with 1GB RAM and a 20GB disk is sufficient for most of the course.

First, install the EPEL, Extra Products for Enterprise Linux, repository on the CentOS 8 system that we will use as the Ansible controller. It is on this system that we install Ansible, and it's the only system that needs any Ansible software explicitly installed.

Listing 1-1. Adding the EPEL Repository on the CentOS 8 Controller
System

```
$ sudo yum install -y epel-release
$ sudo yum update -y epel-release
```

Installing and then updating will ensure that we have the very latest
version of the EPEL repository. A newer version often will exist in the
repository itself. For CentOS, it is this repository from where we can
install Ansible. If using Red Hat, the repository must be enabled via
the subscription manager. This is not anything that you are likely to
be involved with in the exam. I am sure having to deal with candidate
subscriptions is not something Red Hat would want to become involved
with just for the exam.

Next we can install Ansible. It is not a difficult task; let me show you.

Listing 1-2. Install Ansible on CentOS

```
$ yum install -y ansible
```

With Ansible installed, we can take a moment to check the version that
we installed.

Listing 1-3. Printing the Version of Ansible

```
$ ansible --version
ansible 2.9.15
  config file = /etc/ansible/ansible.cfg
  configured module search path = ['/home/tux/.ansible/plugins/
  modules', '/usr/share/ansible/plugins/modules']
  ansible python module location = /usr/lib/python3.6/site-
  packages/ansible
  executable location = /usr/bin/ansible
  python version = 3.6.8 (default, Apr 16 2020, 01:36:27)
  [GCC 8.3.1 20191121 (Red Hat 8.3.1-5)]
```

Reviewing the output, we can see that the EPEL repository has the 2.9.15 version. In the exam you will most likely be using 2.8.x, but there should be little differences.

Installing Ansible on Ubuntu 18.04

It is important, or at least I feel that it is important, that we also learn how to install Ansible on another distribution. Even though Ubuntu will not be used in the exam, in the real world you may want to use Ansible on a distribution other than Red Hat-based. I will step you through the process of installing Ansible on Ubuntu 18.04, but we will only be using the CentOS 8 system as the controller during the course. The Ubuntu system will remain as a managed node for the rest of the course and will not install the Ansible package over these nodes.

Firstly, Ansible is within the standard Ubuntu repositories; however, it is an older version and shows as version 2.5. Although this is OK, it is not really desirable. We can add the software repository directly from Ansible to install something much later. In Debian-based systems, these additional repositories are PPAs or *Personal Package Archives*.

Listing 1-4. Adding the PPA to Ubuntu

```
$ sudo apt update
$ sudo apt install software-properties-common
$ sudo apt-add-repository --yes --update ppa:ansible/ansible
```

Listing 1-5. Install Ansible Where We Add sshpass Also

```
$ sudo apt install ansible sshpass
```

You can also copy this information for the Ansible documentation as well: https://docs.ansible.com/ansible/latest/installation_guide/intro_installation.html#installing-ansible-on-ubuntu.

This will install the latest version from Ansible themselves. Checking the version, we see it is currently the same version in EPEL.

Listing 1-6. Checking the Version Install on Ubuntu

```
$ ansible --version
ansible 2.9.15
  config file = /etc/ansible/ansible.cfg
  configured module search path = [u'/home/tux/.ansible/
  plugins/modules', u'/usr/share/ansible/plugins/modules']
  ansible python module location = /usr/lib/python2.7/dist-
  packages/ansible
  executable location = /usr/bin/ansible
  python version = 2.7.17 (default, Sep 30 2020, 13:38:04)
  [GCC 7.5.0]
```

Remember, we will use the CentOS 8 system as the controller; this Ubuntu host and the other CentOS 8 system will be managed devices. I remind you at this stage that, if you are short on access to systems, it is possible to run most tasks with just the controller. The overall effect, though, is more impressive if we can configure multiple systems with single command. If you can run two or three systems, then it is better.

Summary

Do you know what? You are amazing. You now know what Ansible is and you understand your path to becoming an RHCE, a certified administrative god! Most importantly, you know that you are going to get there by lots of practice. I am guessing that you are so enthusiastic that you are already building your three labs systems. Yes, that is right: two CentOS 8 systems and one Ubuntu 18.04 system. None of the systems need a GUI desktop, which also means resources can be quite minimal on each system. To be honest, 1GB RAM and a 20GB disk is more than enough for each system when only running in console mode. For one chapter we will need 2GB RAM on the controller.

You should have Ansible installed now on a CentOS 8 system. This will act as your Ansible controller. Ansible is an agentless configuration management system, giving the advantage of not having to add supporting software or clients to your managed devices. You also learned that you can install Ansible on other systems if you don't have CentOS 8. The behavior of Ansible is the same, no matter which system is the controller. In the exam, you should be familiar with using CentOS 8 or RHEL 8.

CHAPTER 2

Working with the Ansible Configuration

The configuration file for Ansible controls how the system configuration utility, Ansible, will operate on the managed devices. This may include the way in which rights are escalated and the user account to use in making the connection to the managed device. Do these need to be the same on every project that you work with? Should individual administrators or developers have control over their own configuration? These are good questions, and questions we will try to answer here. Let's look at both the contents of the configuration, what can go into an Ansible configuration file, and the hierarchy of configurations that can be made and their search order.

Note   The effective configuration for Ansible can be determined from the command **ansible --version**. Run this command from the directory in which you would execute the other Ansible commands for your project.

© Andrew Mallett 2021
A. Mallett, *Red Hat Certified Engineer (RHCE) Study Guide*,
https://doi.org/10.1007/978-1-4842-6861-2_2

Ansible Configuration Hierarchy

The full path to the default Ansible configuration file installed along with Ansible is: */etc/ansible/ansible.cfg*. Ansible needs only to be installed on the Ansible controller host system, our main CentOS 8 box. By reading the full output of the version option, we can see the Ansible configuration that is effective based on the current working directory and shell variables.

Listing 2-1. Listing the Current and Default Location for the Ansible Configuration

```
$ pwd
/home/tux
$ ansible --version
ansible 2.9.15
  config file = /etc/ansible/ansible.cfg
  configured module search path = ['/home/tux/.ansible/plugins/
  modules', '/usr/share/ansible/plugins/modules']
  ansible python module location = /usr/lib/python3.6/site-
  packages/ansible
  executable location = /usr/bin/ansible
  python version = 3.6.8 (default, Apr 16 2020, 01:36:27)
  [GCC 8.3.1 20191121 (Red Hat 8.3.1-5)]
```

Directly after the Ansible version number, we see the *config path* directive. This is shown as */etc/ansible/ansible.cfg*. As mentioned before, this is the default location for the file. It is also the fallback location and the very bottom layer of the configuration hierarchy. Having a central location in the */etc* structure would make for a very prescriptive Ansible configuration. Needing to have administrative rights to the controller to modify files within */etc*, you would not expect everyone to edit this file. If no other file could be used, then these settings would be the same for each Ansible project on the controller. Now, I can't argue with that because

I don't know the Ansible project or projects that you are working with; however, often more flexibility will be required and often a configuration for each project is more preferable to centralized configuration. Devolution of power is king where Ansible is concerned.

The effective Ansible configuration is applied on the *first found – first applied* basis. It is important to note that only one configuration can be active and applied and that these configurations are NOT cumulative. The search order is shown in the following bulleted list, with the search from the top of the list to the bottom. The least effective configuration is the */etc/ansible/ansible.cfg* at the bottom of the list.

- **ANSIBLE_CONFIG**: If the environment variable, *ANSIBLE_CONFIG*, is set, then this configuration is used. Default options are used for any configuration option not set. This default behavior is common with all configurations.

- **ansible.cfg**: If there is an *ansible.cfg* file in the current working directory (CWD), AND the ANSIBLE_CONFIG environment variable has not been set, then it is this file that is used.

- **~/.ansible.cfg**: If no previously listed configuration is detected, Ansible will check the current user's home directory for a hidden file called *.ansible.cfg*. If the file exists, then it becomes the third choice within the hierarchy. This is a great option for a user to create, acting as a default for all user projects except those needing a little tweaking. Those needing tweaks can have a configuration file added to the project directory; alternatively, as you will learn, variables can be set to overwrite certain options as can settings within Ansible Playbooks. So, there are lots of options to tweak the configuration as needed.

- */etc/ansible/ansible.cfg*: The default file where no other configuration is in place or detected. The file itself only contains comments, meaning that there are no effective settings from the file. Don't despair though; this will result in the default settings being applied for all settings. The file itself is not wasted, acting as great documentation for the configuration files that you may want to implement.

As a simple demonstration of how we can build up the hierarchy, we can add files to their locations starting from the base of the configuration tree and moving up. Obviously, the base of the tree is in place, as we have already seen with the initial **ansible --version** output. The default *ansible.cfg* is installed along with Ansible.

With only this default file present, you can be certain that it will be used. Using the awesome command **grep**, we can filter the results to see only the line that we are interested in.

Listing 2-2. Listing the Default Configuration Location

```
$ ansible --version | grep 'config file'
  config file = /etc/ansible/ansible.cfg
```

When there is the hidden Ansible file in the user's home directory, it will be the effective file if no other files exist in the later hierarchy. By adding the *$HOME/.ansible.cfg* file, we can see how we start to ascend the hierarchy.

Listing 2-3. Adding a Configuration to the Home Directory

```
$ touch ~/.ansible.cfg
$ ansible --version | grep 'config file'
  config file = /home/tux/.ansible.cfg
```

Moving to level 3 of the hierarchy by adding an *ansible.cfg* file to the current working directory, we can see it take over the effective settings. The *ansible.cfg* in the CWD is the effective configuration for Ansible commands in the absence of the *ANSIBLE_CONFIG* environment variable. In the following code listing you will see that a new directory is created inside our home directory. We move into the newly created directory and create the new empty *ansible.cfg* file. While this directory is our working directory for any Ansible command, it is this file that is used for the configuration in the absence of the variable.

Listing 2-4. Adding a Configuration to the Current Directory

```
$ mkdir $HOME/ansible
$ cd $HOME/ansible
$ touch ansible.cfg
$ ansible --version | grep 'config file'
  config file = /home/tux/ansible/ansible.cfg
```

Important   It is very important for Ansible security that a configuration file is never loaded from a world-writable directory. If a directory is world writable, (where *others* have the write permission), it is possible that a rogue ansible.cfg file is added to your working directory by another user either deliberately or by mistake.

To demonstrate the security issue that we could face, we will now change the permissions on the *$HOME/ansible* directory that we just created, adding in world-writable permissions. Once we have proved that the theory is true, we revert the permissions on the directory, enabling Ansible to read the configuration from the directory.

Listing 2-5. Test Ansible Security

```
$ cd $HOME/ansible
$ chmod -v 777 $HOME/ansible.
mode of '/home/tux/ansible' changed from 0775 (rwxrwxr-x) to
0777 (rwxrwxrwx)
$ ansible --version | grep 'config file'
[WARNING]: Ansible is being run in a world writable directory
(/home/tux/ansible), ignoring it as an ansible.cfg source.
For more
information see https://docs.ansible.com/ansible/devel/
reference_appendices/config.html#cfg-in-world-writable-dir
  config file = /home/tux/.ansible.cfg
$ chmod -v 775 $HOME/ansible
mode of '/home/tux/ansible' changed from 0777 (rwxrwxrwx) to
0775 (rwxrwxr-x)
$ ansible --version | grep 'config file'
  config file = /home/tux/ansible/ansible.cfg
```

At the very top of the configuration hierarchy, we have the environment variable, *ANSIBLE_CONFIG*. This is the big boss of the configuration world and what she says matters; she talks and Ansible listens!

This variable could be set within a login script for a user or dynamically configured at the command line. If it is set within the login script by an administrator, it is worth making the variable read-only, thus eliminating any chance of the variable being changed by the user. For example, if we want to force the configuration to the *ansible.cfg* file in the user's home, we can implement the variable.

Listing 2-6. Using the Variable to Set the Configuration Location
and Viewing Read-Only Variables

```
$ touch $HOME/ansible.cfg
$ declare -xr ANSIBLE_CONFIG=$HOME/ansible.cfg
$ ansible --version | grep 'config file'
  config file = /home/tux/ansible.cfg
$ declare -xr ANSIBLE_CONFIG=$HOME/my.cfg
-bash: declare: ANSIBLE_CONFIG: readonly variable
$ unset ANSIBLE_CONFIG
-bash: unset: ANSIBLE_CONFIG: cannot unset: readonly variable
```

Note   The option **-x** to **declare** sets an environment variable,
(available to all commands) and the option -r sets the variable to be
read-only. As read-only, the variable cannot be unset or changed.
Now, I know you will be used to the **export** command; we could
use **export** to make a variable available to the environment and the
readonly command to make the variable read-only. However, using
the **declare** command affords us the ability to set both options in
the one command execution.

We can see from the examples that as we traverse up the hierarchy,
we use new configurations and ignore those previously used, such as the
default *ansible.cfg*. We can also see that, as administrators, we can enforce
the use of the variable's location by understanding the use of the **declare**
command in the *bash* shell.

For the moment, we do not want to use the variable; we can't unset
this, as we have seen already, but we can log out and log back into the
system. We have not set this in a login script, so this will effectively
clear the variable. We will also delete the *ansible.cfg* file from the home
directory–NOT the hidden file, just the *$HOME/ansible.cfg*.

Listing 2-7. Cleaning the Environment, We Should See the Hidden File as the Effective Configuration When Executed with Home as the Working Directory

```
$ exit
Log back in as tux
$ rm $HOME/ansible.cfg
$ cd $HOME; ansible --version | grep 'config file'
  config file = /home/tux/.ansible.cfg
```

Printing the Ansible Configuration

Even though we have not made any configuration settings as yet, we are still able to print the contents of the effective file, which will be empty. We will also be able to print the effective settings, that is, the default settings. For this, we have access to the command **ansible-config**, which has a stunning three subcommands:

- *ansible-config view*: Print the contents of the current effective Ansible configuration.

- *ansible-config dump*: Print the effective settings, which are made up from explicit settings from the effective files and the default settings where an option is unset.

- *ansible-config list*: This fully details the settings that can be made, either through variables or via directives in the configuration file or Playbook.

It is amazingly easy to see this in action, which I will demonstrate to you. Don't forget to work diligently on your own lab system, the more practice that you can get with these commands, the clearer they become in your mind. The exam is also practical based, meaning that hands-on experience really does matter both for the exam and your own success.

Listing 2-8. Printing the Current Configuration File Content; This Should Be Empty

```
$ cd
$ ansible-config view
```

The *view* subcommand only will print effective settings from the current configuration; any commented lines will not be printed. We can test this by renaming the *$HOME/.ansible.cfg*. This should make the file, */etc/ansible/ansible.cfg*, the effective configuration again as we fall back to the default file. Even though the file is not empty, each line is commented so nothing is printed.

Listing 2-9. Printing the Default Configuration

```
$ mv $HOME/.ansible.cfg $HOME/.ansible.old
$ ansible --version | grep 'config file'
  config file = /etc/ansible/ansible.cfg
$ ansible-config view
$ head -n 15 /etc/ansible/ansible.cfg
# config file for ansible -- https://ansible.com/
# ===================================================

# nearly all parameters can be overridden in ansible-playbook
# or with command line flags. ansible will read ANSIBLE_CONFIG,
# ansible.cfg in the current working directory, .ansible.cfg in
# the home directory or /etc/ansible/ansible.cfg, whichever it
# finds first

[defaults]

# some basic default values...

#inventory      = /etc/ansible/hosts
#library        = /usr/share/my_modules/
```

The configuration takes the form of an INI file, meaning that configuration options are grouped together within section headers in square brackets. The section headers in the default files are not commented, so these are easy to print independently. This is also great practice using regular expressions, which we can use with our good friend **grep**. The regular expressions metacharacters that we use in the query are listed and explained in the following bulleted list:

- **^** : Line starts with

- **\[** : We are literally looking for lines that start with an opening bracket. We need to escape the bracket, as it would be interpreted as a start of a range in a regular expression.

- **.*** : The period in a regular expression represents any character, and the asterisk represents any amount of the previous character. In this way we can say the brackets can contain any number of any character.

- **\]** : Again, we must escape the closing bracket, as we want it to read as a literal and not a regular expressions metacharacter.

- Using **grep**, we are looking to print lines that start with a section header indicated by the header name inside of square brackets.

Listing 2-10. Cataloging the Headers

```
$ grep -E '^\[.*\]' /etc/ansible/ansible.cfg
[defaults]
[inventory]
[privilege_escalation]
[paramiko_connection]
```

```
[ssh_connection]
[persistent_connection]
[accelerate]
[selinux]
[colors]
[diff]
```

So, we have now gained some understanding of the configuration file and the **ansible-config** command. As yet though, we have only seen the *view* subcommand. We must move on now and take a look at the *dump* subcommand. This shows us the current configuration based on explicit settings and those unset and using the default options.

Listing 2-11. Listing the Current Effective Settings

```
$ ansible-config dump | head
ACTION_WARNINGS(default) = True
AGNOSTIC_BECOME_PROMPT(default) = True
ALLOW_WORLD_READABLE_TMPFILES(default) = False
ANSIBLE_CONNECTION_PATH(default) = None
ANSIBLE_COW_PATH(default) = None
ANSIBLE_COW_SELECTION(default) = default
ANSIBLE_COW_WHITELIST(default) = ['bud-frogs', 'bunny',
'cheese', 'daemon', 'default', 'dragon', 'elephant-in-snake',
'elephant', 'eyes', 'hellokitty', 'kitty', 'luke-koala',
'meow', 'milk', 'moofasa', 'moose', 'ren', 'sheep', 'small',
'stegosaurus', 'stimpy', 'supermilker', 'three-eyes', 'turkey',
'turtle', 'tux', 'udder', 'vader-koala', 'vader', 'www']
ANSIBLE_FORCE_COLOR(default) = False
ANSIBLE_NOCOLOR(default) = False
ANSIBLE_NOCOWS(default) = False
```

There are no options currently set in the effective configuration file. Each option we see printed with the *dump* subcommand will show the corresponding default configuration value. This is shown with the use of *(default)* following the configuration name. We have only listed the first ten lines, but each setting would be at its own default setting until we create our own custom configurations.

Although the *dump* subcommand is awesome in its ability to see the current effective settings, it does not provide any help or explanation to the configuration setting. For this, we will need to employ the *list* subcommand. Come on, let's take a look; but we will filter the output to see just one setting. The output is verbose, very verbose, so filtering on a single setting will be easier to see and understand.

Listing 2-12. List All Configuration Settings with Documentation

```
$ ansible-config list | grep -A8 DEFAULT_REMOTE_USER
DEFAULT_REMOTE_USER:
  default: null
  description: [Sets the login user for the target machines,
  'When blank it uses the connection plugin''s default,
  normally the user currently executing Ansible.']
  env:
  - {name: ANSIBLE_REMOTE_USER}
  ini:
  - {key: remote_user, section: defaults}
  name: Login/Remote User
```

The option name is *DEFAULT_REMOTE_USER*; there is no default value for this, but the current user will be used with the Linux plug-in. The value can be set with an environment variable, *ANSIBLE_REMOTE_USER*, or from the configuration value using the key *remote_user* in the defaults section header. The variable, if set, will take precedence over the configuration file.

> **Note**   These commands are of great help to you, as they are available to use in the exam. So, make use of that when needed, and make sure you practice these commands so you are fluent when in the exam.

Creating a Basic Ansible Configuration File

Now, by this stage you must be itching to begin your own configuration. Your voice has been heard and this is what you will now start learning. By making settings within our home directory and the .ansible.cfg file, these can act as default settings for ourselves if they are not set within the working directory. First, we resurrect the *.ansible.cfg* file we previously renamed.

Listing 2-13.   Restoring the .ansible.cfg file in Our Home Directory

```
$ cd ; mv .ansible.old .ansible.cfg
$ ls -la .ansible.cfg
-rw-rw-r--. 1 tux tux 0 Nov 16 14:42 .ansible.cfg
```

We can now set some configuration options that we may want to share across multiple Ansible projects. These settings may be best suited to being configured in the *.ansible.cfg* in the home directory. We begin by making sure we have the correct section headers by copying them from the default file.

> **Note**   Adding the section headers in this way eliminates typos that can occur, and it does not matter that we have sections that are unused.

Listing 2-14. Creating an Ansible Configuration

```
$ grep -E '^\[.*\]' /etc/ansible/ansible.cfg > $HOME/.ansible.
cfg
$ vim $HOME/.ansible.cfg
[defaults]
remote_user = ansible ; we will later create this account
inventory = $HOME/inventory ; list of remote hosts
[inventory]
[privilege_escalation]
become = true ; user rights will be elevated
become_method = sudo ; by using sudo
[paramiko_connection]
[ssh_connection]
[persistent_connection]
[accelerate]
[selinux]
[colors]
[diff]
```

Note   Comments that start a new line can be either the octothorpe (#) or the semicolon (;). Inline comments placed at the configuration line end and commenting the rest of the line have to be made using the semicolon, as we use in this example.

With our brand new configuration in place and waiting to be used, we will be able to demonstrate a little more using the previous **ansible-config** command. It is also important to never assume that what we have typed into the file was correct; a little testing never hurt anyone.

Listing 2-15. Viewing the Configuration

```
$ ansible-config view
[defaults]
remote_user = ansible
inventory = $HOME/inventory
[inventory]
[privilege_escalation]
become = true
become_method = sudo
[paramiko_connection]
[ssh_connection]
[persistent_connection]
[accelerate]
[selinux]
[colors]
[diff]
```

We do have to take care with this command, as there is absolutely no checking of the section headers we have used or of the key or values supplied. The file will print as long as it matches the INI file format. Checking the effective settings with the **dump** subcommand is so much more useful, especially when we filter with the **--only-changed** option. Come on; I will show you.

Listing 2-16. Viewing Settings Changed from the Default

```
$ ansible-config dump --only-changed
DEFAULT_BECOME(/home/tux/.ansible.cfg) = True
DEFAULT_BECOME_METHOD(/home/tux/.ansible.cfg) = sudo
DEFAULT_HOST_LIST(/home/tux/.ansible.cfg) = ['/home/tux/
inventory']
DEFAULT_REMOTE_USER(/home/tux/.ansible.cfg) = ansible
```

The output now also confirms that the settings are valid and usable by Ansible. If the key or header is not recognized, then it does not change anything and the section header or setting is not effective. If we find that we do not see the option or options that we are looking for within the output, it is likely that our fat fingers have got somewhat in the way of perfection.

Summary

The way that I see the current situation is that you are well on your way to becoming an Ansible superhero. Yes, you—officially an Ansible superhero. But perhaps we need to focus more on the exam; after all, that is where the big bucks are. You are well on your way to the acing the exam; just take a look at the facts and start understanding that you can now configure Ansible. You know the hierarchy of configuration that is applied. Starting from the top down, we first search:

- ANSIBLE_CONFIG

- ansible.cfg in CWD so long as the directory is not world-writable

- $HOME/.ansible.cfg

- /etc/ansible/ansible.cfg

Not only that, in this chapter you learned how to view and print the configuration. First, you learned to use the **ansible --version** command to print the path to the configuration and the dedicated command **ansible-config** to print settings. With this we have three subcommands: *view*, *dump* and *list*, with perhaps **ansible-config dump --only-changed** being one of the most useful and my personal favorite. And yes, I do have fat fingers!

When creating our own custom configurations, we may use comments. At the start of a new line we may comment the complete line using either the # or the ;. Whereas, if we need to comment the rest of a line, we are limited to using the semicolon. We used this knowledge to create a simple configuration within our home directory. So, of course, the file name was hidden and created as *.ansible.cfg* and adding settings that we could use across projects, overwriting them for specific projects either with their own project-based configuration or with environment variables. We can now move on to further our knowledge by looking at creating host inventories that we have already referenced from our configuration.

CHAPTER 3

Creating an Ansible Inventory

When working with Ansible on our CentOS 8 controller, we can target hosts that we want to manage directly via a list of hosts. This list can be provided as an option to the **ansible** command. Certainly though, we can do better than this. Rather than an ad hoc list, we will want to create a persistent file-based list of hosts. This list is the Ansible inventory and within the file we can also define groups based around geography, function, or operating system, making it easy to target hosts specifically. Inventory files provide the consistency that we need when targeting hosts, no matter if we are working directly at the command line or from Playbooks.

Note   I know we have not introduced Playbook yet, but don't worry, we will soon. In the meantime, a Playbook is a text file written in YAML format that describes the tasks that should be executed on managed devices: a manifest of work to be done, if you like.

© Andrew Mallett 2021
A. Mallett, *Red Hat Certified Engineer (RHCE) Study Guide*,
https://doi.org/10.1007/978-1-4842-6861-2_3

Creating an Inventory

Having created a configuration for Ansible already in the previous chapter, we can almost certainly proceed with the next tasks in managing host lists with Ansible and creating the inventory. Within the Ansible configuration the item name for the location of the inventory file is *DEFAULT_HOST_LIST*. Using **grep**, we can display the documented help on this setting using the output from **ansible-config list**.

Listing 3-1.   Gaining Help in the Host List or Inventory

```
$ ansible-config list | grep -A10 DEFAULT_HOST_LIST
DEFAULT_HOST_LIST:
  default: /etc/ansible/hosts
  description: Comma separated list of Ansible inventory
  sources
  env:
  - {name: ANSIBLE_INVENTORY}
  expand_relative_paths: true
  ini:
  - {key: inventory, section: defaults}
  name: Inventory Source
  type: pathlist
  yaml: {key: defaults.inventory}
```

One of the first things that we should notice from the output is the default value to this key; it is the file */etc/ansible/hosts*. Although this file does not contain any effective entries, again, each line being commented, it does provide great and usable examples. When you are new to the inventory and inventory groups, this is a great starting point. The default file is in the INI format but, as we will see later, we can also use YAML format for inventory files if we wish. To display the examples from this file without the other commented lines, we can look for lines that start with a double comment; further to this, we can remove the comments from the display by piping the output to the **tr** command. Where our desire to become creative at the command line overwhelms, we can additionally use the command **tee** to both display the output to the screen as well as populating our own inventory file. I will show you, but only if you promise to practice yourself on your own system.

Listing 3-2. Listing the Default Inventory File to Populate Our Own Inventory

```
$ grep '^##' /etc/ansible/hosts | tr -d '##' | tee ~/inventory
green.example.com
blue.example.com
192.168.100.1
192.168.100.10
[webservers]
alpha.example.org
beta.example.org
192.168.1.100
192.168.1.110
www[001:006].example.com
[dbservers]
db01.intranet.mydomain.net
db02.intranet.mydomain.net
10.25.1.56
10.25.1.57
db-[99:101]-node.example.com
```

Note   If you want to gain a better understanding of the command in the previous pipeline, then build the commands up. Start first by listing the file without filters:

```
$ cat /etc/ansible/hosts
$ grep '^##' /etc/ansible/hosts
$ grep '^##' /etc/ansible/hosts | tr -d '##'
$ grep '^##' /etc/ansible/hosts | tr -d '##' | tee ~/inventory
$ cat ~/inventory
```

Without any work, (this is always a great way to start), we now have an inventory with groups that we can practice with. For us, this is an awesome start to understand the inventory files and the associated tool that we can use to query the inventory. I am guessing the IP Addresses used do not meet your network and they certainly do not match my hosts, so we will replace this file, or at least its contents, later, after our initial practice in querying the inventory.

Query Inventory Entries

We have two commands that we can use to print entries from the inventory file. These include the **ansible** command as well as the specific **ansible-inventory** command. In addition to any groups that we explicitly define within the file, we have two built-in groups:

- *all*: Yes, you have guessed it, the group *all* refers to all hosts contained in the inventory file.

- *ungrouped*: The *ungrouped* group refers to those hosts not included in any specific inventory group within the file.

You probably will be using the group *all* much of the time in Ansible. Very often we will want to target all hosts; after all, that is why you added them to the inventory. As yet, I have never had the need to target the *ungrouped* group, but there is still time! First let's make sure that we are working in the home directory of our user, and we will check the Ansible configuration that is in use. We want to be certain that the inventory file we are using is set to *$HOME/inventory*.

Listing 3-3. Verify the Ansible Configuration

```
$ ansible --version | grep 'config file'
  config file = /home/tux/.ansible.cfg
$ ansible-config dump --only-changed
DEFAULT_BECOME(/home/tux/.ansible.cfg) = True
DEFAULT_BECOME_METHOD(/home/tux/.ansible.cfg) = sudo
DEFAULT_HOST_LIST(/home/tux/.ansible.cfg) = ['/home/tux/
inventory']
DEFAULT_REMOTE_USER(/home/tux/.ansible.cfg) = ansible
```

Note   If you are not seeing the same configuration, your time may be well spent by reviewing the previous chapter where we created the configuration file ~/.ansible.cfg. The book is not going away, I assure you; we will be here waiting for you on your return.

Listing Inventory Hosts Using Ansible

Having the Ansible configuration file in place and having ensured that the inventory file used is the file we created, we are ready to go. The simplest way that we can list all hosts within the inventory is to use the **ansible** command. Using the built-in group *all*, each host will be listed.

Listing 3-4. Listing Hosts with the Ansible Command, Some Output Is Trimmed to Reduce Space Used in This Book, Thereby Not Just Saving Trees but Saving Your Eyes!

```
$ ansible all --list-hosts
  hosts (21):
    green.example.com
    blue.example.com
    192.168.100.1
    192.168.100.10
    alpha.example.org
    beta.example.org
    www001.example.com
    www002.example.com
    www003.example.com
    db-99-node.example.com
    db-100-node.example.com
    db-101-node.example.com
```

We can also list groups and their members; using the *webservers* group instead of the *all* group demonstrates this.

Listing 3-5. List Specific Groups with Ansible

```
$ ansible webservers --list-hosts
  hosts (10):
    alpha.example.org
    beta.example.org
    192.168.1.100
    192.168.1.110
    www001.example.com
    www002.example.com
    www003.example.com
```

```
www004.example.com
www005.example.com
www006.example.com
```

If you recall, we have two built-in groups. We have seen the listing of all inventory hosts and now we can see the group, *ungrouped*, those hosts not included in a named group.

Listing 3-6. Listing Hosts That Do Not Exist in Any Named Group

```
$ ansible ungrouped --list-hosts
  hosts (4):
    green.example.com
    blue.example.com
    192.168.100.1
    192.168.100.10
```

Listing Hosts Using Ansible-Inventory

Even though the **ansible** command is quite simple, as we progress through the course, we will begin to realize that listing only the hosts is limited. Often there will be inventory variables that we also need to view. It is times like these, when our needs become more complex, that we can rely on the **ansible-inventory** command. Again, as before, we can begin by listing all hosts in the inventory. The default output is in JSON format, but I have included the option to print in YAML because it is less verbose.

Listing 3-7. Listing All Hosts with the ansible-inventory Command, Some Output Is Trimmed to Reduce Space Used

```
$ ansible-inventory --list --yaml
all:
  children:
    dbservers:
      hosts:
        10.25.1.56: {}
        10.25.1.57: {}
        db-100-node.example.com: {}
        db-101-node.example.com: {}
    ungrouped:
      hosts:
        blue.example.com: {}
        green.example.com: {}
    webservers:
      hosts:
        www001.example.com: {}
        www002.example.com: {}
        www003.example.com: {}
```

We can see the brace-brackets against each host; this is where inventory variables can be displayed if any are set. We are not using any at the moment, but I can show you how useful the **ansible-inventory** command can be in listing these variables. Taking a working configuration that I have on my own systems, I can first list all hosts with **ansible** and then **ansible-inventory**.

Note   The following command is run on my internal Ansible controller used for deployment of AWS systems. These entries are not within your own inventory currently, but we will start to use variables soon in the lab inventory.

Listing 3-8. Listing Inventory with Variables, First with ansible and Then ansible-inventory

```
$ ansible all --list-hosts
  hosts (1):
    3.8.123.144
$ ansible-inventory --list --yaml
all:
  children:
    redhat: {}
    suse:
      hosts:
        3.8.123.144:
          admin_group: sudo
          ansible_user: ec2-user
    ubuntu: {}
    ungrouped: {}
```

We can see that the host has two variables that have been configured: the *admin_group* and the *ansible_user*. The *admin_group* variable will be used when creating users that need to administer the system; the group may differ from Linux distribution to Linux distribution. Some distributions use the group *wheel* and some use the group *sudo*. In AWS the default user account that you should connect as differs based on who created the image; in openSUSE it is the *ec2-user* and in CentOS it is the *centos* user account. By implementing a variable we are able to cater for the differing accounts. Variables in Ansible help us deal with these differing needs and, as administrators, being able to see the variables will help us debug issues with Ansible commands and Playbook execution.

Working back on the CentOS 8 controller as our lab system, we can use **ansible-inventory** to list hosts in just a single group, just as we could with **ansible**.

Listing 3-9. Listing Group Membership with ansible-inventory

```
$ ansible-inventory --graph --yaml dbservers
@dbservers:
  |--10.25.1.56
  |--10.25.1.57
  |--db-100-node.example.com
  |--db-101-node.example.com
  |--db-99-node.example.com
  |--db01.intranet.mydomain.net
  |--db02.intranet.mydomain.net
```

Adding Host and Group Entries

When we add hosts to the inventory file, we can use the resolvable hostname or IP address. We can also add ranges for both hostnames or IP addresses.

Listing 3-10. Adding Ranges to the Ansible Inventory

```
# To add www1.example.com, www2.example.com, www3.example.com
www[1:3].example.com
# To add a range of IP addresses
192.168.1.[1:5]
```

When adding in groups, the group name will be added to a section header. For example, to add a group for London we can add the following line to the inventory file. Members of the group should be listed below the group section header.

Listing 3-11. Adding a Group to the Ansible Inventory

```
[London]
```

We can also make great use of nested groups in the inventory file. Nested groups are groups listed in other groups. For example, if we have a *London* group and *Bristol* group defined in the inventory, we can nest these groups in the *UK* group. The keyword *children* is used to indicate that the members are nested groups.

Listing 3-12. Using Nested Groups in the Ansible Inventory

```
[London]
server1
server3
[Bristol]
server2
server4
[UK:children]
Bristol
London
```

Discovering Hosts on Your Network

If you are using an internal NAT network for VMWare, then you will know that you have a limited number of hosts running on that network. If, like me, the only virtual machines that you are running on that NAT network are the three hosts that you want for this course, then we can make some magic happen. We can do this through port scans, and to start we will need to install the port scanner **nmap**.

Listing 3-13. Installing the Port Scanner nmap on the Controller

```
$ sudo yum install -y nmap
```

Using the port scanner on our NAT network, we can detect hosts that are both running on the network and listening on TCP port 22, the SSH port. We will need the SSH port to connect from Ansible. When scanning the network, make sure that you enter the network address for your network, but do not scan the network if you are not authorized to do so!

Important   In some companies scanning of networks may trigger alerts, as a network scan may be the precursor of a cyber attack on the network and server resources. If this is not your own personal network, it is imperative that you have prior written agreement to run the scan. There is nothing dangerous in the commands that we run in the example, but of course we are discovering services on the network that could be viewed as recognizance.

Listing 3-14. Scanning the Network for SSH Servers

```
$ sudo nmap   -Pn -p 22 -n 172.16.120.0/24 --open -oG -
Nov 18 16:51:36 2020 as: nmap -Pn -p 22 -n --open -oG -
172.16.120.0/24
Host: 172.16.120.185 ()  Status: Up
Host: 172.16.120.185 ()  Ports: 22/open/tcp//ssh///
Host: 172.16.120.188 ()  Status: Up
Host: 172.16.120.188 ()  Ports: 22/open/tcp//ssh///
Host: 172.16.120.161 ()  Status: Up
Host: 172.16.120.161 ()  Ports: 22/open/tcp//ssh///
# Nmap done at Wed Nov 18 16:51:41 2020 -- 256 IP addresses
(6 hosts up) scanned in 5.57 seconds
```

The port scan that we initiate has several options designed to give us the best output for our needs. The options are listed as follows:

- **-Pn**: Don't probe the host initially to see if it is up. As we are discovering a single port, this will not slow the scan and may prove more accurate.

- **-p 22**: Only scan port 22; we default to TCP.

- **-n 172.16.120.0/24**: We are scanning the NAT network in my case.

- **--open**: Only list the result if the port is open, as opposed to filtered or closed.

- **-oG -**: We make the output more easily filtered by commands such as **grep**; the final dash indicates that we send the output to STDOUT, the screen.

The results that we see are OK but, if you recall, we want to create an inventory file from this output. This means that we need to exclude the rest of the data shown in the output. We can choose the command **awk** to both filter the lines that we want and the exact field that we want. We want to look for lines that contain *22/open* and we want to return just the second field, which is the IP address of the host on the network.

Listing 3-15. Extracting IP Addresses

```
$ sudo nmap -Pn -p22 -n 172.16.120.0/24 --open -oG - | awk
'/22\/open/{ print $2 }'
172.16.120.185
172.16.120.188
172.16.120.161
```

The final step is to send the output to the inventory file once we have validated it on the screen; if it looks OK, send it to the *$HOME/inventory* file. To be certain all is well with the world and the inventory file, we list the contents of the file with **ansible-inventory**.

Listing 3-16. Dynamically Creating Our Own Inventory

```
$ sudo nmap -Pn -p22 -n 172.16.120.0/24 --open -oG - | awk
'/22\/open/{ print $2 }' | tee $HOME/inventory
$ ansible-inventory --list --yaml
all:
  children:
    ungrouped:
      hosts:
        172.16.120.161: {}
        172.16.120.185: {}
        172.16.120.188: {}
```

Inventory Variables

For this chapter we will conclude by setting host and group variables that can be used alongside the inventory. The variables can be added directly to the standard INI style inventory; however, these variables become a little clearer when abstracted from the inventory and stored in separate files. This makes the inventory file less dense and the variables more modular.

By default, Ansible uses native OpenSSH to connect to managed devices. OpenSSH is preferable on Linux- and Unix-based systems because it supports ControlPersist, Kerberos authentication, and options stored in *~/.ssh/config* such as Jump Host setup. If your controller system uses an older version of OpenSSH that does not support ControlPersist, Ansible will fall back to a Python implementation of OpenSSH called *paramiko*. Other connection methods are available, such as WinRM for

Microsoft Windows systems. We may also want to skip the use of SSH when managing the controller itself; we can use a local connection. To manage this, we can use a variable assigned to the controller host. This, as we previously mentioned, can be set on the INI file inventory. You will need to determine the IP address of your controller to be able to add the variable to the host.

Listing 3-17. Determine the Controller IP and Configure Variable for Local Connection

```
$ cd
$ ip -4 addr show
1: lo: <LOOPBACK,UP,LOWER_UP> mtu 65536 qdisc noqueue state
UNKNOWN group default qlen 1000
    inet 127.0.0.1/8 scope host lo
       valid_lft forever preferred_lft forever
2: ens33: <BROADCAST,MULTICAST,UP,LOWER_UP> mtu 1500 qdisc
fq_codel state UP group default qlen 1000
    inet 172.16.120.161/24 brd 172.16.120.255 scope global
    dynamic noprefixroute ens33
       valid_lft 1425sec preferred_lft 1425sec
$ sed -Ei 's/(172.16.120.161)/\1 ansible_connection=local/'
inventory
$ ansible-inventory  --yaml --host 172.16.120.161
ansible_connection: local
```

Although this does work, and we can add more variables to this host, you will find that your inventory becomes denser and less easy to read. Keeping the inventory separate from the variables is a tidier way of working. Let's use **sed** to revert the setting that we just added to the inventory.

Listing 3-18. Reverting the Inventory

```
$ cd
$ sed -Ei 's/\<ansible_connection=local\>//' inventory
$ ansible-inventory --yaml --host 172.16.120.161
{}
```

The brace-brackets for the selected host are now empty, indicating that there are no host variables in place. We will now create two subdirectories; these need to be created in the same directory as the inventory file—in this case, the home directory of our user account. With the directories created, one for host and one for groups, we can add in YAML files for hosts or groups that need variables configured.

Listing 3-19. Separate Inventory and Variables

```
$ cd
$ mkdir {host,group}_vars
$ echo "ansible_connection: local" > host_vars/172.16.120.161
$ ansible-inventory  --yaml --host 172.16.120.161
ansible_connection: local
```

Note   The separated variable files are in YAML format; the keys are delimited from their value with a **:** and a **<space>**. We can see it in this newly created file: **ansible_connection: local**, whereas in the INI inventory file, the key/value pair use the **=** sign, so **ansible_connection=local**.

Summary

I am simply blown away with your progress. You are now able to effectively configure the Ansible inventory, the list of hosts that we can manage. Not only this, you have been able to create variables to be used with hosts or groups. This is truly amazing, and you are going to find this strong foundation in Ansible really useful moving on from this.

In working through this chapter, we also learned more command line tips that can help speed up our use of the bash shell. First, we added some **sed** examples to dynamically edit files. The stream editor, **sed**, is very useful and works in a similar way to **grep**; with **sed** though, we can edit files and not just filter output. As well as using both **sed** and **grep** in the chapter, we also looked at **awk**, the big brother to both of these commands. Second, when creating the directories for the variable files, we created both directories with the one command by using the brace-brackets. The command **mkdir {host,group}_vars** will expand into **mkdir host_vars; mkdir group_vars**. These shortcuts can make you quicker at the command line, and time is of the essence in the exam.

You are also able to query the inventory using both the **ansible --list-hosts** command and the **ansible-inventory** command. If you simply meed to list groups or all hosts, then use the former command. The latter command is great to list variables associated with hosts or groups.

45

CHAPTER 4

Using Ad Hoc Commands and Ansible Preparation

I am beginning to feel your impatience growing; yes, it even transcends the time and distance between us. You want to learn Ansible and gain great hands-on experience with the product. Well, I have great news for you; you do not have to wait any longer. We are about to unleash the scorching power kept from you thus far. You are about to learn how to configure the three lab systems in parallel with the execution of a single command on the Ansible controller. Ad hoc commands allow us to dive straight into Ansible without the need of Playbook files. This makes them paradoxically both good and bad. Ad hoc commands are good because they can be quickly executed when and as needed. They are bad because the commands that we execute lack the repeatably correct attribute associated with YAML Playbooks. With a Playbook, the file is a persistent manifest of the tasks that need to be executed, both documenting the configuration and achieving the nirvana of any configuration management system: being *repeatably correct*. With ad hoc commands we may easily omit a required configuration parameter, but this will not happen with a Playbook. We will

© Andrew Mallett 2021
A. Mallett, *Red Hat Certified Engineer (RHCE) Study Guide*,
https://doi.org/10.1007/978-1-4842-6861-2_4

get the same results each time the Playbook is executed. I am guessing that you now understand the term "ad hoc" in relationship to Ansible. These commands will be run on an as needed basis and will not necessarily need to be repeated.

Testing Ansible

Although we have been as busy as the proverbial bee in creating the configuration and inventory, we have not yet seen Ansible at work. Simple configuration changes are at the heart of where ad hoc commands prevail, and they are executed with our good friend the **ansible** command. The simplest of these commands is the Ansible *ping* module. It is not a network ICMP ping but connects using the *ansible_connect* method to discover if a Python interpreter exists on the managed device. The connection will normally be SSH but, as we have seen, we have set the controller to use a local connection. By checking that we can run the *ping* module on the managed host against our inventory hosts, we will be able to check that everything is working adequately and correct issues that may arise. We can then continue to configure the systems in the desired state for the rest of the course.

Note   We assume that you are logged in to the controller as the **tux** user account who has the ability to run all commands as root using **sudo**. The **tux** account should also exist on the managed devices with the ability also to run commands with **sudo**.

Listing 4-1. Testing Ansible with the Python Ping Module

```
$ ANSIBLE_REMOTE_USER=tux ansible all -k -K -m ping
SSH password:
BECOME password[defaults to SSH password]:
        172.16.120.188 | FAILED! => {
    "msg": "Using a SSH password instead of a key is not
    possible because Host Key checking is enabled and sshpass
    does not support this.  Please add this host's fingerprint
    to your known_hosts file to manage this host."
    }
        172.16.120.185 | FAILED! => {
    "msg": "Using a SSH password instead of a key is not
    possible because Host Key checking is enabled and sshpass
    does not support this.  Please add this host's fingerprint
    to your known_hosts file to manage this host."
}
        172.16.120.161 | SUCCESS => {
    "ansible_facts": {
        "discovered_interpreter_python": "/usr/libexec/
        platform-python"
    },
    "changed": false,
    "ping": "pong"
}
```

Green is good and red is not so good. We have also needed to add in a heap of switches that we can later omit once the configuration of the managed hosts is complete. We will cover the switches shortly, but first let's correct the error that we see. For me the controller IP address shows as connecting successfully; it's the remote systems where we use SSH that have failed. If we read the message, we can see the cause. Yes, don't just freeze like a rabbit caught in headlights—read the error message! We have not previously connected using SSH to the remote systems and do not have their public keys stored as SSH *known_hosts*. We can take two approaches here: either use **ssh-keyscan** to collect the remote keys or, as we will do, we can choose to disable host key checking. In our lab environment this is a sage choice. Let's copy the configuration into our CWD and adjust it to suit our needs.

Listing 4-2. Overwriting the Effective Ansible Configuration

```
$ mkdir -p $HOME/ansible/setup
$ cd !$
cd   $HOME/ansible/setup
$ cp ~/.ansible.cfg .
$ ansible --version | grep 'config file'
  config file = /home/tux/ansible/setup/ansible.cfg
```

Note   We have used the **!$** variable to represent the last arguments used at the command line to make changing directories easier and quicker.

Editing this file can both correct the error we have seen and improve the efficiency of command execution. Within the original file, we have set the option to elevate privileges; for the ping module, we do not need to run as root, meaning that we do not need to enter the sudo password (**-K**). We also use the remote account, *ansible*, in the original file, which we have not yet created. Choosing to modify this setting in the configuration will mean that we do not need to overwrite the setting with the variable. We must not forget that we should correct the error also; adding the key **host_key_ checking** with a value of **false** will resolve this issue. We should edit the file so it looks similar to this. The changes made to the file are highlighted.

Listing 4-3. Modified $HOME/ansible/setup/ansible.cfg

```
[defaults]
remote_user = tux
inventory = $HOME/inventory
host_key_checking = false
[inventory]
[privilege_escalation]
become = false
become_method = sudo
```

There is also an advantage in using the setting **become = false**; we can raise privileges with ad hoc commands using the option **-b** but not the reverse. Not escalating unnecessarily makes the system more secure as a benefit. Having edited the file with our favored text editor, we are ready to go. Let us now test the settings are effective before rerunning the Ansible ping.

Listing 4-4. Testing the Configuration Is Effective and Running the Ping

```
$ ansible-config dump --only-changed
DEFAULT_BECOME(/home/tux/ansible/setup/ansible.cfg) = False
DEFAULT_BECOME_METHOD(/home/tux/ansible/setup/ansible.cfg) =
sudo
DEFAULT_HOST_LIST(/home/tux/ansible/setup/ansible.cfg) = ['/
home/tux/inventory']
DEFAULT_REMOTE_USER(/home/tux/ansible/setup/ansible.cfg) = tux
HOST_KEY_CHECKING(/home/tux/ansible/setup/ansible.cfg) = False
$ ansible all -k -m ping
...
```

We should now have three successful green outputs, one for each host. If you are using an Ubuntu 18.04 system, as I am, you will see a warning about the Python interpreter being detected as */usr/bin/python* rather than */usr/bin/python3*. We can fix this by setting Ubuntu 18.04 hosts to use Python 3 by adding an inventory variable, but we will come back to that. Let's first make sure we understand the options used in the command line execution of ad hoc commands. The following list shows some command options:

- **all**: The argument specifies the group in the inventory that we want to target. We are using the **all** group here.

- **-k**: Prompt for the SSH password. We will later use key-based authentication, allowing us to omit this option.

- **-K**: We have already omitted this, as we did not need escalation for the ping module to succeed. Where we do need escalation, ideally the user account will have passwordless access to sudo. We will configure this with an ad hoc command.

- **-b**: Use privilege escalation even if it is not set in the configuration.

- **-m**: The name of the Ansible Python module to execute. We use the ping module.

- **-a**: Not used or needed here. We can, and often need to, supply arguments to the module and this is supplied with the -a option.

Implementing Ansible Inventory Groups

From the warning previously generated by the Ubuntu 18.04 system regarding the Python interpreter, we can start to see the need for groups already. Although, we could set a host variable for that host, it is likely that we will have more 18.04 hosts enlisted in the future and adding groups now will save work in the future. Setting the required variable against the group will be easier to understand and is likely to be more accurate, where no host is forgotten. At this stage we will create groups for the CentOS hosts and an Ubuntu group. We will also create a group for 18.04 hosts, as it is likely that version 20.04 of Ubuntu will not need the same variable setting. We will use the code name for 18.04 hosts of *bionic* for the group name. Group names should not start with a number. We can nest the bionic group in the Ubuntu group. This is easy to implement as we will see now. Make sure that you can determine the IP address of the Ubuntu system, so it is added to the correct group.

Listing 4-5. Modify Your $HOME/inventory File to Include Groups

```
$ cat $HOME/inventory
[bionic]
172.16.120.188
[centos]
172.16.120.161
172.16.120.185
[ubuntu:children]
bionic
$ ansible bionic --list-hosts
  hosts (1):
    172.16.120.188
$ ansible ubuntu --list-hosts
  hosts (1):
    172.16.120.188
```

```
$ ansible centos --list-hosts
  hosts (2):
    172.16.120.161
    172.16.120.185
```

Setting the groups enables the mechanism of targeting these groups independently in ad hoc commands. We do not have to only use the group *all*. We can also use the groups to set the required variables. In the following we first list the bionic group without the variable being configured before setting the variable and relisting the group before rerunning the ping command targeting the Ubuntu group only.

Note   We can still use the **--host** option to reference a group name with the command **ansible-inventory**.

Listing 4-6.   Implementing Group Variables to Resolve Ad Hoc Issues

```
$ ansible-inventory --host bionic --yaml
{}
$ echo "ansible_python_interpreter: /usr/bin/python3" > $HOME/
group_vars/bionic
$ ansible-inventory --host bionic --yaml
ansible_python_interpreter: /usr/bin/python3
$ ansible ubuntu -k -m ping
SSH password:
172.16.120.188 | SUCCESS => {
    "changed": false,
    "ping": "pong"
}
```

Using both CentOS and Ubuntu allows us to uncover issues that we would not see with a single distribution. This was mentioned within the introduction to the lab systems, but it is worth repeating because we have been able to investigate additional options useful in a disparate environment that is common to Ansible deployments. This has also allowed us to cement our understanding of groups and nested groups early on in the course.

Preparing the User Account for Ansible

The reality is that using a dedicated account for Ansible operation on the managed systems allows for greater transparency and security for the configuration changes. We have used the *tux* account so far and we will need to continue with this account until we create the dedicated account for Ansible.

Creating the User

We will create the account directly using the *user* module. We will need arguments to create the user, enabling us to demonstrate the **-a** option. We set the user password as an argument, which needs to be an encrypted hash. We generate this hash prior to creating the account. Having stored the encrypted password in a variable, we can run the ad hoc command, needing to elevate privileges by using the option **-b**. We also need to prompt for both the SSH password and sudo password using the options **-k** and **-K**, respectively. Having created the account, we can confirm that entries exist in both the *passwd* and *shadow* databases.

Listing 4-7. Using an Ad Hoc Command to Create the Dedicated Ansible User Account

```
$ user_password=$(openssl passwd -6 Password1)
$ ansible all -kKbm user -a "name=ansible password=$user_
  password"
...
$ getent passwd ansible
ansible:x:1001:1001::/home/ansible:/bin/bash
$ sudo getent shadow ansible
ansible:$6$li9wmHhZW/TUHYeX$WzH596QutESoI5j3GYqoqnkSLlN.
9VxdnMt5aix7SX18AE.1.3rH25quQU1wLrtg3zwXCNNdlQ8Bm6CenJenL/
:18586:0:99999:7:::
```

Allowing Passwordless Sudo Access

When using the newly created account, we will need to elevate privileges without adding a password. This helps streamline the operation, especially if we want to schedule the Ansible commands to run unattended. Adding a file to the */etc/sudoes.d/* directory on our Linux systems will enable access to **sudo** without a password. We create a local file and then distribute it using the Ansible *copy* module. We can validate the file before we distribute it, to maintain the integrity of the sudoers subsystem.

Listing 4-8. Allowing Access Without a Password to sudo

```
$ cd ~/ansible/setup
$ echo "ansible ALL=(root) NOPASSWD: ALL" > ansible
$ sudo visudo -cf ansible
ansible: parsed OK
$ ansible all -bkK -m copy -a "src=ansible dest=/etc/sudoers.d/
  ansible"
```

SSH-Key Authentication

We would also prefer to use key-based authentication, making the account more robust as well as reducing the need for interaction when executing commands. We need to generate an SSH key-pair for out user account, tux. The public key will need to be distributed to remote systems and the Ansible account. Authentication from the tux user to the ansible user account without the need of a password for SSH. The Ansible module we will use to distribute the key is the authorized_key module, but first we need to generate the key pair for tux.

Listing 4-9. Establishing Key-Based Authentication

```
$ ssh-keygen
Generating public/private rsa key pair.
Enter file in which to save the key (/home/tux/.ssh/id_rsa):
Enter passphrase (empty for no passphrase): (leave blank)
Enter same passphrase again: (leave blank)
Your identification has been saved in /home/tux/.ssh/id_rsa.
Your public key has been saved in /home/tux/.ssh/id_rsa.pub.
The key fingerprint is:
SHA256:BdooIqc1yJbyIlEC20U/Xqxvx4k7AGqWasvWeTj64wo tux@
controller
The key's randomart image is:
+---[RSA 3072]----+
|o=*o+   ..       |
+----[SHA256]-----+
$ ansible all -bkKm authorized_key -a "user='ansible'
  state='present' \
 key='{{ lookup('file','/home/tux/.ssh/id_rsa.pub')}}'"
...
```

The output from the three systems should be in yellow, indicating that changes have taken place. We are very nearly complete in our configuration. I wonder though if you have been able to think of an issue that we still may have.

Well, it is quite simple, with two changes needed. We need to tell Ansible to use the dedicated *ansible* account we have created, and we need to ensure that the controller, where we use the local connection from the *tux* user, allows passwordless **sudo** access.

Configuring the Final Changes

Listing 4-10.   Configuring the tux Account on the Controller System and Reverting the ansible.cfg

```
$ cd ~/ansible/setup ; cp ansible tux
$ sed -i s/ansible/tux/ tux
$ sudo visudo -cf tux
tux: parsed OK
$ sudo cp tux /etc/sudoers.d/tux
$ sed -i s/tux/ansible/ ansible.cfg
```

We can now test this by reexecuting the previous **ansible** command that distributed the SSH key. We should now be able to exclude all password prompts. Reexecuting the command will not cause any issues, Ansible is *idempotent*, meaning that we can run the same ad hoc command many times and changes will only be implemented where we do not meet the desired state of configuration. We should see green output for each host, indicating that we are in compliance with the configuration.

Listing 4-11. Testing Access Without Interaction

```
$ ansible all -bm authorized_key -a "user='ansible'
state='present' \
 key='{{ lookup('file','/home/tux/.ssh/id_rsa.pub')}}'"
...
```

Gaining Help on Modules

We have made great progress in this chapter and made use of the *ping*, *copy*, *user*, and *authorized_key* modules. The question is: how do you know what modules exist and what arguments they take? This is another simple but great question that we can answer with the **ansible-doc** command. In the following code examples, we first see how to print all modules; we also count them to see that we have over 3,000 in the version that we are using. After that we gain help on the user module introduced in this chapter.

Listing 4-12. List All Ansible Modules

```
$ ansible-doc --list
...
$ ansible-doc --list | wc -l
3387
```

Listing 4-13. Gain Help on a Specific Ansible Module

```
$ ansible-doc user
```

When gaining help on a module, you can search for *EXAMPLES* to gain practical guides on how the module can be used. They include YAML Playbook examples, but these are easily adapted to the command line. We can extend our practice on the command line with ad hoc commands by adding and removing another user.

Listing 4-14. Adding a Supplementary Test User to Our Systems

```
$ ansible all -bm user -a "name=fred"
```

When working with the user module the state is assumed to be *present* if we do not specify the key. The following command is identical to the previous listing where we did not define the state. Then output will be green, indicating that we are compliant with the configuration; the user exists.

Listing 4-15. Explicitly Setting the State in the User Module

```
$ ansible all -bm user -a "name=fred state=present"
```

When removing a user account, we set the state to be *absent*. We can also set to remove their home directory and mail spool file with the *remove=true* key/value pair.

Listing 4-16. Removing a User Account and Their Home Directory

```
$ ansible all -bm user -a "name=fred state=absent remove=true"
```

Summary

We are really able to use Ansible now and use it well. Already you will be able to see how effective your management of systems can be. We easily created the new account on the three systems, and added the sudo file and our authentication key. Each command that we executed was performed on the *three managed hosts*. Even with the configuration that we needed to implement, performing just these tasks will have been quicker with Ansible than configuring each host individually. This is just the start; the benefits grow exponentially from this point on.

In this chapter we added groups to our inventory and added the variable *ansible_python_interpreter* for the *bionic* group, Ubuntu 18.04. We also made it easy to automatically accept SSH host keys within the Ansible configuration using the key *host_key_checking* with a false value. Where we are often connecting to new hosts such as within an agile DevOps environment, this setting is essential. With the configuration and inventory in place we were quickly able to extend our Ansible knowledge, where we could use the *ping* module to check the Python interpreter on the managed devices before using the *user* module to create a dedicated account for Ansible to use. This user will need access to sudo without a password, and we used the *copy* module to deliver the sudoers file to each host before using the *authorized_key* module to allow key-based authentication to the user account we added.

At the end of this chapter, I really hope that you are building your confidence in configuration management with Ansible. Don't forget that your confidence is going to be built with practice. So please practice the commands in your own labs and investigate the help you can find with the **ansible-doc** command.

CHAPTER 5

Writing YAML and Basic Playbooks

Ad hoc commands in Ansible are awesome; look how we were able to easily create the user account across all three systems. However, we must not let ourselves become too caught up in the excitement of what we have achieved; ad hoc commands were part of our journey but not the destination. So, let us celebrate that which we have achieved but not rest too long; we will move forward and begin our understanding of Playbooks and the basics of YAML. The first thing to understand is the acronym itself: **Y**AML **A**in't **M**arkup **L**anguage. It is for data processing and not a markup language. The next and most important feature to understand and master is the use of significant leading whitespace. The indentation level of an element dictates the relationship with other elements in the file.

In this chapter you will learn to write Playbooks, and benefit from repeatable commands that are correct on each execution. We will learn to tune our text editors for YAML files, helping us create correct YAML syntax. We will also have a sneak peek at a graphical editor and Microsoft Visual Studio Code on Linux. Remember, the Ansible controller could well be a Linux workstation, making it quite reasonable to use a GUI to write YAML. Strap yourself in securely, as we are about to launch your next level of learning.

© Andrew Mallett 2021
A. Mallett, *Red Hat Certified Engineer (RHCE) Study Guide*,
https://doi.org/10.1007/978-1-4842-6861-2_5

Writing Simple YAML Playbooks

When creating Playbooks we need to be aware that, as with Python files, we are dealing with a file format where leading whitespace is significant and has a meaning. To keep the file format clean and uncluttered, we do not use any form of brackets to group related code elements; we use the indent level. You may look at a file and each element may appear to be lined up correctly with previous elements. If one line uses a tab as an indent and another line uses eight spaces, they are not at the same indent level. It is best that you use explicit spaces and not tabs; using the tab key still becomes convenient, so being able to configure your text editor to treat tabs as spaces is a great setting to learn. First, we must understand what makes up a Playbook.

Elements of a Playbook

We know Playbooks are YAML files, but what exactly do they contain, especially, what *must* they contain? My dear friend and reader, this is simple: a Playbook will contain at least one play and a play will contain at least one task. An Ansible task relates to each individual ad hoc command we could execute from the command line:

- *Playbook*: YAML formatted text file containing one or more plays

- *Play*: The play will contain one or more tasks and later we will see additional elements, such as handlers.

- *Tasks*: A task will represent the execution of a module with arguments, either optional or mandatory, as we would use with ad hoc commands. The modules we use in Playbook tasks are exactly the same Python modules that would be used with ad hoc commands.

This is a benefit over competitive systems such as Salt from SaltStack. Salt uses different modules for remote execution (ad hoc commands), compared with state modules, where Salt state files are comparable to Playbooks.

Our First Playbook

The best way to learn Playbook construction is to actually get our keyboards dirty and start writing one. That's so much better than just discussing what a Playbook could look like. So, let's make this first Playbook useful and look at installing software, something that we have not previously looked at with ad hoc commands. We will continue to use the *$HOME/ansible/setup* directory for the project. Please do use the command line text editor that you are most happy to use. Mine is **vim**, but we will later look at customizing both **vim** and **nano** to work well with YAML.

Listing 5-1. Creating Our First Playbook

```
$ cd $HOME/ansible/setup
$ ansible-config dump --only-changed
DEFAULT_BECOME(/home/tux/ansible/setup/ansible.cfg) = False
DEFAULT_BECOME_METHOD(/home/tux/ansible/setup/ansible.cfg) = sudo
DEFAULT_HOST_LIST(/home/tux/ansible/setup/ansible.cfg) =
['/home/tux/inventory']
DEFAULT_REMOTE_USER(/home/tux/ansible/setup/ansible.cfg) = ansible
HOST_KEY_CHECKING(/home/tux/ansible/setup/ansible.cfg) = False
$ vim software.yml
---
- name: My first play
  hosts: all
```

```
become: true
tasks:
        - name: Install software
          package:
                  name: bash-completion
                  state: present
...
```

In the text file we have created, we have one Playbook containing one play. That play, in turn, contains just the single task.

- *Playbook*: The Playbook is the document itself. YAML documents will optionally start with three dashes, **---**, and the corresponding document end marker is the three dots, **...**. Sadly, we do not have any reference to the three amigos, which would be slightly more amusing. A Playbook will contain at least one play. These are represented as a list. List items in YAML are designated with the single dash, **-**.

- *Play*: Within each play we set the optional name. Although optional, I would strongly advise adding a name to both help document the file and help with diagnostics. The play name is printed as part of the output to our console. At the same level as the play **name** key, we set other keys for the individual play. These keys must be at the same indent level as the **name** key. That is, lining up with the letter **n** from **name** and NOT the dash. We can see that **name**, **hosts**, **become**, and **tasks** are all elements of this play being vertically aligned. Within the play the **hosts** key is used to reference the inventory hosts to target. The **become** key is used to force elevation of privileges in a similar way to the **-b** option to an ad hoc command. Finally, we have the **tasks** dictionary. Unlike a standard YAML key, which stores a single value, a YAML dictionary contains multiple keys and values or, as in this case, stores a list of key/value pairs in the form of individual tasks.

- *Task*: Living beneath the **tasks** dictionary, each task needs to indent to the same level of other tasks within the same dictionary. We use the default eight spaces used by vim as indentation. Each task is a list item to the tasks dictionary, so the optional task name is prefaced with the dash and space. Within the task we make use of the **package** Ansible Python module, akin to the module name we would specify with the **-m** option in an ad hoc command. The module is a YAML dictionary containing a collection of key/ value pairs. Those keys need to be indented to show their relationship to the package dictionary. We are consistent with the eight spaces used to indent these keys. With the module we reference the name of the package to work with and the state. Here we dictate that it should be installed with the state **present**. We could use **absent**, **present**, or **latest** to ensure the package is up to date.

Note   Although we do have a **yum** module and an **apt** module, using the **package** module to manage software allows Ansible to be agnostic towards the operating system choosing the most suitable packager. Although we strive for Ansible Playbooks to be agnostic, we do need to take care with the package name, which may differ from OS to OS. Group variables can help us overcome these differences. In this case, the package has the same name on both CentOS and Ubuntu.

Now, at this stage, you should create the Playbook file, *software.yml*, within the *$HOME/ansible/setup* directory. Take great care to observe the indentation levels we have referenced. Once you have created the file, you can execute it. You may, optionally, choose to check the syntax prior to execution. Instead of the **ansible** command we have used with ad hoc execution, we now utilize the **ansible-playbook** command.

Listing 5-2. Checking Playbook Syntax and Executing Playbooks, Executed from $HOME/ansible/setup

```
$ $ ansible-playbook software.yml --syntax-check

playbook: software.yml
$ ansible-playbook software.yml
PLAY [My first play]
TASK [Gathering Facts]
ok: [172.16.120.185]
ok: [172.16.120.188]
ok: [172.16.120.161]
TASK [Install software]
ok: [172.16.120.188]
ok: [172.16.120.161]
changed: [172.16.120.185]
```

From the output of the Playbook execution, which has been slightly abbreviated for greater clarity, we can see that on both CentOS hosts that no changes were necessary; however, the package was not present and thus installed on the Ubuntu system. All hosts are now in the desired state. We could execute the same Playbook again to these hosts and none of the systems would need to install the software. Looking closely, we can now start to understand why we should not treat the play or task names as optional. It both helps to document the file and the Ansible output. But, but, hang on, there are **two tasks**; we only created a single task, yet two tasks are executed. What is Ansible playing at! Ah, great question and I am glad you noticed. The *Gather Facts* task will collect facts or information about the managed device that we can use within the play. This might be for logic in deciding which tasks should execute or for including some fact such as the hostname of the system within a task. If we will not use facts within the play, we can disable this task with the play key: **gather_facts: false**.

Tip   Disabling the fact collection will speed the execution of the play and is worthwhile when facts are not required for the individual play. Having multiple plays within a Playbook will mean multiple executions of the *gather_facts* task, one for each play, if not disabled. Try to group tasks that require facts into a single play when using more than one play.

Extending the Playbook Using Facts

I am not sure as to how you are feeling, but I am exploding with excitement about how much Ansible can and does save me time. Installing software is essential to me. I run many online training courses on AWS. Being able to deploy brand new, clean AWS systems and have them configured with the packages I need for specific courses is invaluable. I regularly configure ten or more systems for a course, and I use Ansible because it is agentless and works effortlessly on new systems. As a side note, my personal Ansible controller is a Raspberry Pi that is always powered on in my home office in Peterborough, UK.

We can begin to extend the Playbook by adding in a second task to simply display the hostname of the managed system. We can use the **debug** module for this. Also, don't be too dismayed by this; although it is not useful in itself, we can become accustomed to using facts.

Listing 5-3. Using Facts in the Playbook

```
---
- name: My first play
  hosts: all
  become: true
  tasks:
          - name: Install software
            package:
                    name: bash-completion
                    state: present
          - name: Show hostname
            debug:
                    msg: "This host is {{ ansible_hostname }}"
...
```

Using the **debug** module and the **msg** key, we are able to print text to the output shown on our console. Variables, including facts, must be included in double-quoted text strings and surrounded with double brace-brackets as shown in the code. For each host this is executed upon, we will see both the static text and the hostname of the managed device being printed on the controller. Both tasks will run, but only the **Show hostname** task will result in action, as the software from the first task is already installed.

Listing 5-4. Viewing Abbreviated Output from the Debug Module

```
$ ansible-playbook software.yml
TASK [Show hostname]
ok: [172.16.120.161] => {
    "msg": "This host is controller"
}
ok: [172.16.120.185] => {
    "msg": "This host is client"
```

```
}
ok: [172.16.120.188] => {
    "msg": "This host is ubuntu"
}
```

To list all facts on a host, we can use an ad hoc command and the
setup module. This could also be run from a Playbook but is most suited
to an ad hoc command that provides a quick, once-only reference. We
have excluded output from the following example due to its verbosity, but
please, do run the command and view the output on your own systems.

Listing 5-5. Listing All Facts from the Targeted Group or Host

```
$ ansible ubuntu -m setup
```

Installing Multiple Packages

If, like me, you have your favored software that is needed on each system, you
will want to ensure that they are omnipresent. We can install many packages
with a single task execution of the package module, creating a list of package
names. We will now edit the file to include more packages in the initial task.

Listing 5-6. Installing More Than One Package

```
$ cat $HOME/inventory
$ vim software.yml
---
- name: My first play
  hosts: all
  become: true
  tasks:
          - name: Install software
            package:
```

```
                    name:
                            - bash-completion
                            - vim
                            - tree
                            - nano
                    state: present
          - name: Show hostname
            debug:
                    msg: "This host is {{ ansible_hostname }}"
...
```

$ **ansible-playbook software.yml**
```
TASK [Install software]
changed: [172.16.120.161]
changed: [172.16.120.188]
changed: [172.16.120.185]
```

Note   In using multiple package names in this manner, we only use the underlying package once and it would be similar to **yum install curl vim tree**, etc. If we used multiple tasks, extra time and resources are used, as it becomes similar to running **yum install curl**, **yum install tree,** and so on. We are able to make both the Playbook and its execution more efficient.

Improving Text Editors

When we look at the developing YAML file we have been working with, the real estate needed both on the screen and the book to display it is increasing. Much of this is because of the default indent level of eight spaces. YAML files will be easier to work with if we set this to a smaller amount, together with other options we can use to speed their editing. First, we will look at customizing the **nano** text editor, as the defaults in CentOS don't allow for any help with YAML files. The final edit to the *software.yml* file should have installed **nano** on all systems where it was needed. We will create a *.nanorc* file in our own home directory on the controller.

Listing 5-7. Creating the $HOME/.nanorc Control File for the Nano Text Editor

```
$ nano $HOME/.nanorc
set autoindent
set tabsize 2
set tabstospaces
```

Configuring this control file allows efficient editing of YAML files by ensuring that we return to the previous indent level with the use of the return key. We set the tab key to use two spaces and convert tabs to be saved as spaces. We can test it by creating a simple test Playbook within the setup directory we have been using previously. When using lists, the **autoindent** option will return the cursor to the level used by the dash of the list item. We will need to use the tab key to indent a further two spaces lining up with the list item rather than the dash. This changes the indent level so the next use of the return key will position the cursor at the correct level. This is one reason to use a tab stop of two spaces in YAML files.

Listing 5-8. Sample Playbook File to Test .nanorc

```
$ cd $HOME/ansible/setup; vim nano.yml
---
- name: Ping
  hosts: all
  gather_facts: false
```

```
tasks:
  - name: Ping hosts
    ping:
...
```

Using **vim**, you may have found that you had some assistance in the editing. Being at the default the result may not have been the best, but there are huge improvements that we can make. Returning to our home directory, we can edit the *.vimrc* file so that it reads similar to the example shown:

Listing 5-9. Sample $HOME/.vimrc File for Editing YAML Files

```
$ vim $HOME/.vimrc
set tabstop=2 shiftwidth=2 expandtab autoindent
set cursorcolumn cursorline
```

The first line provides for very similar effects as in the previous *.nanorc* file we created earlier. The second line of the new *.vimrc* file is really very useful in any format where the indent level is significant, such as the YAML Playbook that we will be working with. We highlight the vertical column where the cursor is positioned, and the current horizontal line is underlined. You may find that the column highlighting may not work on your terminal, depending on the terminal emulation implemented. The default PuTTY terminal does not work with the setting but can be adjusted. It will be fantastic if you knew exactly what you should be seeing when editing files with these new settings. So, with no thought to the expense, the great folk at Apress have included the following screen capture. This capture was taken while editing the previous *nano.yml* file. The highlighted column is currently on the list of tasks, the dash. We can use this visual tool to ensure that a consistent indentation is used correctly throughout the YAML file. As the YAML becomes longer, this feature becomes increasingly useful.

```
 ---
 - name: Ping
   hosts: all
   gather_facts: false
   tasks:
     - name: Ping hosts
       ping:
 ...
```

Figure 5-1. *Editing YAML files with vim and new .vimrc file*

Going All GUI

If we are using a graphical desktop for the controller, we can make use of quite powerful IDEs, integrated development environments, to edit the Playbooks. Using an Ubuntu desktop that includes Microsoft's Visual Studio Code in the standard repositories, and editing the previously shown Playbook, we can see some of the benefits of the IDE.

```
home > tux >  ! nano.yml > {} 0 > [ ] tasks > {} 0 > [●] ping
1    ---
2    - name: Ping
3      hosts: all
4      gather_facts: false
5      tasks:
6        - name: Ping
7          ping:
```

Figure 5-2. *Editing YAML files in Visual Studio code*

Summary

As we draw this chapter into the deepening red skies of our expertise, we should recall how this chapter will shape our success and career. Being able to create repeatable configurations for new deployments and continuous compliant deployments is a feature accessible to us through Ansible Playbooks. Written in YAML format, they both document the configuration and enforce compliance with your described needs.

Features of a YAML document include the document header shown with three dashes and the document footer with triple periods.

- `---`: YAML document header shown with three dashes

- `...`: Similarly, in YAML three periods indicate the document footer.

Lists in YAML are shown with a single dash. We have seen lists used with the lists of plays in a Playbook and the list of tasks within a play. We have also seen that we can install multiple packages with a list of package names.

Listing 5-10. List of Package Names Used with the Ansible Package Module

```
package:
  name:
    - bash-completion
    - vim
    - tree
    - nano
  state: present
```

Working with YAML files, we have learned the need to understand and format the indent level to group related items together. Configuring our text editor to store tabs as spaces can help ensure that we are able to make these configurations more easily and accurately.

Rather than using the **ansible** command to execute Playbooks, we make use of the **ansible-playbook** command with the option of syntax checking. Both commands make use of the same inventory and ansible configuration. Consider setting your configuration file not to elevate privileges, as it is easy to elevate from within an Ansible play. Often the most important reminder is to look at the documentation of a module with the ansible-doc command and dig out their *EXAMPLES* section.

CHAPTER 6

Managing Users with Ansible Playbooks

Although we have already created a new user with an ad hoc command, we haven't done the same with a Playbook. Creating users within a Playbook definition means those ad hoc steps become more prescriptive and will happen in the same way on each execution, importantly, without omissions. Even though our three hosts have the dedicated Ansible user account, we can provision new systems as they come online in a consistent manner using Playbooks.

In this chapter you will learn to write Playbooks to both add and remove users and even see how we can use a single Playbook to both create and delete users with logic to control which task executes. We will revisit group variables to cater to the differences between Ubuntu and CentOS, and spend time investigating how user passwords work and the differences between one-way password hash encryption and encryption mechanisms that can be decrypted. As an RHCE course, I do not want you to miss out on essential security knowledge that you will benefit from learning.

© Andrew Mallett 2021
A. Mallett, *Red Hat Certified Engineer (RHCE) Study Guide*,
https://doi.org/10.1007/978-1-4842-6861-2_6

Playbook to Manage Users

We will begin by remaining in the CWD, the *$HOME/ansible/setup* directory, and start developing a generic Playbook to manage users in general. Later we will begin work on the Playbook to create the dedicated Ansible user account, replicating what we have previously worked on in an ad hoc manner from the CLI. As always, documentation becomes essential to your learning and quick reference in the exam environment. If you only use the documentation when you take the exam, then don't expect to be quick or proficient on accessing that help. Building great experience with **ansible-doc** now will pay huge dividends in the exam, believe me. Take the time to read the complete list of options provisioned by the **user** module and you will gain that broad understanding on how you can use the module to suit your own needs.

User Module Help

As a start, would you humor me and, for your own benefit, research the module that should be used when creating users in the Microsoft Windows OS; this is listed within the **user** module help. Once you have aced that, I would like you to research further into the help to determine how you can disable password-based authentication for a user.

Listing 6-1. Researching User Module Documentation

```
$ ansible-doc user
```

Note   It does not take a lot of time to read the complete user module help. Invest in yourself and read the options available. As a tip though, the module for Windows is shown in the first paragraph. To disable the password, read the help on the *password_lock* key. You can practice with this and other options, observing their behavior.

Creating a Consistent User Account

We have already created a dedicated user account for the account Ansible, but was it consistently created in the same way across each system? I am guessing your answer is either "I don't know" or "I guess so." Well, that is not good enough is it; yes or no? These accounts *should* be the same and they are likely to be the same across the same OS. We are using two distributions, and where we have used both CentOS and Ubuntu the consistency is less likely to be the same unless each option for a user has been set. To demonstrate where user defaults vary, let's run a new module that accesses the shell running a command with arguments. We can list the shell associated with each account by listing the seventh field of the */etc/passwd* file for the user.

Listing 6-2. Listing the Default Shell for the Ansible User

```
$ cd $HOME/ansible/setup
$ ansible all -m shell -a "getent passwd ansible | cut -f7 -d:"
172.16.120.161 | CHANGED | rc=0 >>
/bin/bash
172.16.120.188 | CHANGED | rc=0 >>
/bin/sh
172.16.120.185 | CHANGED | rc=0 >>
/bin/bash
```

We have to do a little detective work here, referencing the IP address to the OS, but the two CentOS hosts use */bin/bash* and Ubuntu uses */bin/sh*. Creating an Ansible Playbook to configure the user's shell will modify the existing user, replacing only the fields that need to be updated.

Listing 6-3. Ensuring a Consistent Shell Within a New Playbook

```
$ vim user.yml
---
- name: Manage User Account
  hosts: all
  become: true
  gather_facts: false
  tasks:
    - name: Create User
      user:
        name: ansible
        shell: /bin/bash
        state: present
...
```

Currently in this Playbook, we set just the *name*, default *shell*, and the *state* keys. We could omit the state key, as *present* is the default value for this module, but why would we? Including this, although not required, provides better documentation and uses 14 extra keystrokes, (if I can count). Executing this Playbook will modify the user account in Ubuntu, where bash is not currently the user's default shell.

Listing 6-4. Setting the Default Shell, Ensuring Consistency Across Distributions

```
$ ansible-playbook user.yml
TASK [Create User]
ok: [172.16.120.161]
changed: [172.16.120.188]
ok: [172.16.120.185]
$ ansible all -m shell -a "getent passwd ansible | cut -f7 -d:"
172.16.120.161 | CHANGED | rc=0 >>
```

/bin/bash

```
172.16.120.188 | CHANGED | rc=0 >>
```
/bin/bash
```
172.16.120.185 | CHANGED | rc=0 >>
```
/bin/bash

We can quickly understand how using a Playbook can give us more accurate and consistent results. Even though we can set exactly the same options with ad hoc commands, they become less convenient when more options are required.

Using an Ansible Loop Control

We've also previously seen how we can specify more than one package name within a single task. That option is not available with the user module though. Thinking about why this is the case, we have to understand the underlying commands: **yum** allows for more than one package but **useradd** does not allow for multiple users. We can use **loop** controls in Ansible to overcome this limitation. The **loop** is part of the *task* and not part of the *module*, the alignment is with other task items. The special variable *item* is used as the value to the user module *name* key; the *item* variable is populated by the iterating the **loop** control.

Listing 6-5. Creating Many Users, Edit the Existing Playbook to Support Three New Users

```
$ cd $HOME/ansible/setup
$ vim user.yml
---
- name: Manage User Account
  hosts: all
  become: true
  gather_facts: false
```

```
tasks:
  - name: Create User
    user:
      name: "{{ item }}"
      shell: /bin/bash
      state: present
    loop:
      - user1
      - user2
      - user3
...
```

```
$ ansible-playbook user.yml
TASK [Create User]
changed: [172.16.120.188] => (item=user1)
changed: [172.16.120.188] => (item=user2)
changed: [172.16.120.161] => (item=user1)
changed: [172.16.120.185] => (item=user1)
changed: [172.16.120.188] => (item=user3)
changed: [172.16.120.161] => (item=user2)
changed: [172.16.120.185] => (item=user2)
changed: [172.16.120.161] => (item=user3)
changed: [172.16.120.185] => (item=user3)
```

From the output of the Playbook execution, which has been slightly abbreviated for greater clarity, we clearly see the creation of the three accounts on each system. The Ansible **loop** control can be used with any module and is a real tool within your own armory.

Deleting Users

Clicking just a few keys, we can easily modify the Playbook to delete those same users. We will now quickly delete these user accounts before moving on to look at using variables more creatively.

Listing 6-6. Deleting Users Using Playbooks

```
$ vim user.yml
---
- name: Manage User Account
  hosts: all
  become: true
  gather_facts: false
  tasks:
    - name: Delete User
      user:
        name: "{{ item }}"
        state: absent
        remove: true
      loop:
        - user1
        - user2
        - user3
...
$ ansible-playbook user.yml
```

Note   If you recall from Chapter 4, **remove: true** is used to ensure the user's home directory and associated mail spool and cron files are removed.

Using Variables and Logic with Playbooks

Returning to managing a single user, we can learn how we can become quite inventive in creating and deleting users. By not hard coding the user's name into the Playbook, we can allow more flexibility. We may also want the choice to either create or delete the account. Variables passed to the Playbook at runtime can allow this to happen and easily, as you will soon learn.

In the following edited Playbook, you will notice that I have added two tasks to the single play. As part of each task, I have added a **when** clause that reads the **user_create** variable. Please note that we do not enclose the variable in brace-brackets, as it is the variable is an argument to a clause that expects a variable. The user's name for each task comes from another variable. Both of these variables are passed using the option **-e** to the **ansible-playbook** command.

Listing 6-7. Building Logic and Choice into the Playbook

```
$ vim user.yml
---
- name: Manage User Account
  hosts: all
  become: true
  gather_facts: false
  tasks:
    - name: Create User
      user:
        name: "{{ user_name }}"
        shell: /bin/bash
        state: present
      when: user_create == 'yes'
    - name: Delete User
```

```
user:
  name: "{{ user_name }}"
  state: absent
  remove:   true
when: user_create == 'no'
...
$ ansible-playbook -e user_create=yes -e user_name=mary user.yml
$ ansible-playbook -e user_create=no -e user_name=mary user.yml
```

Executing the Playbook with the correct variables allows us the choice and flexibility so often needed in an agile DevOps work environment.

Managing User Passwords

When setting passwords for users, we are required to provide the encrypted hash of the password in the same way that we would need to with the underlying **useradd** command. Password hashes are encrypted passwords, but a hash is a *one-way encryption* that cannot be decrypted. I feel it is useful for you to know how authentication with these hashes works and the elements of the encrypted password that we see in the /etc/shadow file.

Password Elements

The password stored within the /etc/shadow file contains three elements allowing for authentication against the password hash. These elements are delimited with the dollar symbol. We can extract the shadow information for a user using the **getent** command.

Listing 6-8. Listing a User's Password

```
$ sudo getent shadow ansible | cut -f2 -d:
$6$li9wmHhZW/TUHYeX$WzH596QutESoI5j3GYqoqnkSLlN.9VxdnMt5aix7SX
18AE.1.3rH25quQU1wLrtg3zwXCNNdlQ8Bm6CenJenL/
```

- *Encryption Algorithm*: The first element of the
  password comes directly after the first **$** and before
  the second. We have the value **6** here, indicating we
  use SHA512 encryption to create the hash. A value of **5**
  would use SHA256 and 1 for the weaker MD5.

- *SALT*: This is a SALTED password, meaning that there
  is a randomness added to the password. The SALT is a
  16-byte text string that should be randomly generated.
  The SALT used here comes directly after the second $
  and before the third. The value is:

  li9wmHhZW/TUHYeX . The SALT is combined with the
  entered password and encryption algorithm to create
  the password hash. If the SALT is not randomized, the
  password system is weakened. It would be possible
  to see users with the same password value, perhaps
  accounts that have not been changed from a default
  password.

- *Hash*: The final password follows the third **$** symbol.
  The hash shown here is:

  WzH596QutESoI5j3GYqoqnkSLlN.9VxdnMt5aix7SX18AE.
  1.3rH25quQU1wLrtg3zwXCNNdlQ8Bm6CenJenL/ . Use of
  the same clear text password, SALT and algorithm will
  create exactly the same hash which is the encrypted
  form of the password.

Authenticating Users

The password hash is secure, as it uses a nonreversable crypt mechanism. To authenticate users, we have to compare the hash created from the password that has been entered and used with the SALT from the stored password and the same algorithm. Neither that SALT nor the algorithm is encrypted. We can see this in the following examples; first, we show that when the same password is combined with the default randomly generated SALT, a unique hash is created each time. We then use the same SALT value and we are presented with a consistent hash. This is how authentication works: by checking that same hash is created.

Note   For brevity of output, we use the 128-bit encryption offered by MD5 rather than the much more secure 512 bits of SHA512. This is purely to reduce the display space needed for the smaller key and would not be used in practice.

Listing 6-9. Using OpenSSL to Demonstrate Authentication

```
$ openssl passwd -1 Password1
$1$/EX4F4Hi$YxXViUagixN9DYZ2LvtBM/
$ openssl passwd -1 Password1
$1$7y2QB7Xk$aBdYTlO5vHFYOT61luJeUo
$ openssl passwd -salt 7y2QB7Xk -1 Password1
$1$7y2QB7Xk$aBdYTlO5vHFYOT61luJeUo
```

By using the same SALT from a stored password, the hash produced will be the same if we have entered the same password.

Generating Passwords in Playbooks

Generating passwords within Ansible Playbook utilizes a Python function, **password_hash**. This is quite simple and is demonstrated through a URL link in the help documentation for the **user** module. The big issue here is that within their example a static text SALT is used. This is NOT what you want to do, as it will create the same hash for the same given password. Their example also uses an ad hoc command, but this could easily be adjusted to a Playbook style. Using the **debug** module to print to the screen, we can see the generated hash. In our examples, which follow, we show the Ansible example before adjusting it to use a random SALT. Just as before, we will be using MD5 rather than the more secure SHA512 for reasons of compactness of the output:

- *Example 1*: Uses the static SALT of *mysecret*

- *Example 2*: Uses the same static SALT, and we can see the same hash is produced

- *Example 3*: It's actually simpler to use a random SALT, by excluding the second argument to the **password_ hash** function. This produces a unique hash for the entered password.

Listing 6-10. Using Python to Generate Password Hashes, First with Static SALT and then Random SALT Values

```
$ ansible ubuntu  -m debug -a "msg={{ 'mypassword' | password_
hash('md5', 'mysecret') }}"
172.16.120.188 | SUCCESS => {
    "msg": "$1$mysecret$EOXe5aWuqhm5pgpi4Epcy/"
}
$ ansible ubuntu  -m debug -a "msg={{ 'mypassword' | password_
hash('md5', 'mysecret') }}"
```

```
172.16.120.188 | SUCCESS => {
    "msg": "$1$mysecret$EOXe5aWuqhm5pgpi4Epcy/"
}
$ ansible ubuntu  -m debug -a "msg={{ 'mypassword' | password_
hash('md5') }}"
172.16.120.188 | SUCCESS => {
    "msg": "$1$.GAXnycZ$CZGGRTWc..KKqFijwWJpW1"
}
```

Adding this to the Playbook is child's play for us by this stage. Later in this book, you will see how to protect the clear text password value, which will be stored in the YAML file. As well as adding the **password** key to the Playbook, we will add the key **update_password** so we can avoid resetting a password of a user who has changed their password. We only want to set the default value for new user passwords.

Listing 6-11. Setting Passwords with Playbooks for New User Accounts

```
$ vim user.yml
---
- name: Manage User Account
  hosts: all
  become: true
  gather_facts: false
  tasks:
    - name: Create User
      user:
        name: "{{ user_name }}"
        shell: /bin/bash
        state: present
        password: "{{ 'Password1' | password_hash('sha512') }}"
        update_password: on_create
```

```
      when: user_create == 'yes'
   - name: Delete User
     user:
       name: "{{ user_name }}"
       state: absent
       remove:  true
      when: user_create == 'no'
...
```

We now can manage our user accounts by using the single Playbook to either create or delete the account, as well as understanding the best ways to manage user passwords. I think that we are about ready to create the initial setup of Ansible managed hosts with a Playbook.

Using a Playbook to Create Managed Host Setup

Maybe you have been wondering why we used the directory name *setup* for our project. Well, we have been moving to this point when we can create a single Playbook to run the initial configuration of the Ansible controller and managed hosts. Working in a new Playbook, *$HOME/ansible/setup/setup.yml*, we will build this up in stages, representing the building blocks that we have previously run through as ad hoc commands.

The first task is to generate an SSH key pair for our own user account on the controller. I have been using the user account *tux*. This key is ONLY needed on the controller and we specify this within the *hosts* key of the play, where previously we have used the group *all*. The value of the *hosts* key should be a string, and as we are using an IP address it needs to be quoted to avoid misinterpretation. The user's name can be passed automatically to the Playbook using the shell variable *$USER* representing the logged in user account. We revert to prompting for the **sudo** password assuming that we have not yet set passwordless **sudo** access.

Listing 6-12. Ensuring an SSH Key Pair Exists for the Operator User Account

```
$ vim setup.yml
---
- name: Manage User Account
  hosts: "172.16.120.161"
  become: true
  gather_facts: false
  tasks:
    - name: Update User
      user:
        name: "{{ user_name }}"
        state: present
        generate_ssh_key: true
...
$ ansible-playbook -K -e user_name=$USER setup.yml
BECOME password:
```

I think that you will agree that this is starting to look very good; of course the key pair will be in place, so nothing will need to be changed. Next up, we make sure that we have passwordless **sudo** access. First make sure that you have the file *$HOME/ansible/setup/tux*, being the **sudo** file to allow tux access to **sudo** without needing a password. Make sure that the name used in the file represents the user account that you use on your controller.

Listing 6-13. The tux sudo File

```
$ cat $HOME/ansible/setup/tux
tux ALL=(root) NOPASSWD: ALL
```

With the file ready, we can add the task to the existing play in the *setup.yml.*

Listing 6-14. Adding the Task to Allow sudo Access Without Password on the Controller

```
$ vim setup.yml
---
- name: Manage User Account
  hosts: "172.16.120.161"
  become: true
  gather_facts: false
  tasks:
    - name: Update User
      user:
        name: "{{ user_name }}"
        state: present
        generate_ssh_key: true
    - name: Password-less access for operator
      copy:
        src: tux
        dest: /etc/sudoers.d/tux...
$ ansible-playbook -K -e user_name=$USER setup.yml
```

On our controller this file will already be in place, so we should meet the current configuration.

The next step is to deploy the dedicated account for Ansible to managed devices. We will need a new play allowing us to specify the hosts group *all*. The play will also allow us to set the *remote_user* key to *tux* rather than making changes to the Ansible configuration referring to the *ansible* user account. Additionally, we will configure the group membership for the new user to be a member of the correct administrative group. This will require adjustment to the inventory variables and allows for a great review of the inventory commands.

Listing 6-15. Creating the Inventory Variables and the new
Dedicated Account

```
$ echo "admin_group: sudo" >> ~/group_vars/ubuntu
$ echo "admin_group: wheel" >> ~/group_vars/centos
$ ansible-inventory --yaml --list
all:
  children:
    centos:
      hosts:
        172.16.120.161:
          admin_group: wheel
          ansible_connection: local
        172.16.120.185:
          admin_group: wheel
    ubuntu:
      children:
        bionic:
          hosts:
            172.16.120.188:
              admin_group: sudo
              ansible_python_interpreter: /usr/bin/python3
    ungrouped: {}
$ vim setup.yml
---

- name: Manage User Account
  hosts: "172.16.120.161"
  become: true
  gather_facts: false
  tasks:
    - name: Update User
      user:
```

```
          name: "{{ user_name }}"
          state: present
          generate_ssh_key: true
      - name: Password-less access for operator
        copy:
          src: tux
          dest: /etc/sudoers.d/tux
- name: Manage Dedicated Ansible Account
  hosts: all
  become: true
  gather_facts: false
  remote_user: tux
  tasks:
    - name: Create Ansible Account
      user:
        name: ansible
        state: present
        groups: "{{ admin_group }}"
        password: "{{ 'Password1' | password_hash('sha512') }}"
        update_password: on_create
        comment: Dedicated Ansible Devops Account
        shell: bin/bash
...
$ ansible-playbook -Kk -e user_name=$USER setup.yml
SSH password:
BECOME password[defaults to SSH password]:
```

The Playbook is really coming along now, although we do meet the
configuration needs. By having the Playbook, we can configure new hosts
in exactly the same consistent manner without extra work. Moving on, we
can now enable SSH authentication to the dedicated account using the
authorized_key module.

Listing 6-16. Enabling Key-Based Authentication, Assuming We Are Using the tux Account on the Controller

```
$ vim setup.yml
---
- name: Manage User Account
  hosts: "172.16.120.161"
  become: true
  gather_facts: false
  tasks:
    - name: Password-less access for operator
      copy:
        src: tux
        dest: /etc/sudoers.d/tux
- name: Manage Dedicated Ansible Account
  hosts: all
  become: true
  gather_facts: false
  remote_user: tux
  tasks:
    - name: Create Ansible Account
      user:
        name: ansible
        state: present
        groups: "{{ admin_group }}"
        password: "{{ 'Password1' | password_hash('sha512') }}"
        update_password: on_create
        comment: Dedicated Ansible Devops Account
        shell: /bin/bash
    - name: Install Local User Key
      authorized_key:
        user: ansible
```

```
      state: present
      manage_dir: true
      key: "{{ lookup('file', '/home/tux/.ssh/id_rsa.pub')
}}"
...
$ ansible-playbook -Kk -e user_name=$USER setup.yml
SSH password:
BECOME password[defaults to SSH password]:
```

The final step is to add the passwordless access to **sudo** for the
dedicated Ansible account. For us, we already have the file for the account.
We just need to add the last task to the second play. The completed
Playbook is shown in the following code block.

Listing 6-17. The Final setup.yml

```
$ vim setup.yml
---
- name: Manage User Account
  hosts: "172.16.120.161"
  become: true
  gather_facts: false
  tasks:
    - name: Update User
      user:
        name: "{{ user_name }}"
        state: present
        generate_ssh_key: true
    - name: Password-less access for operator
      copy:
        src: tux
        dest: /etc/sudoers.d/tux
- name: Manage Dedicated Ansible Account
  hosts: all
```

```
become: true
gather_facts: false
remote_user: tux
tasks:
  - name: Create Ansible Account
    user:
      name: ansible
      state: present
      groups: "{{ admin_group }}"
      password: "{{ 'Password1' | password_hash('sha512') }}"
      update_password: on_create
      comment: Dedicated Ansible Devops Account
      shell: /bin/bash
  - name: Install Local User Key
    authorized_key:
      user: ansible
      state: present
      manage_dir: true
      key: "{{ lookup('file', '/home/tux/.ssh/id_rsa.pub')
}}"
  - name: Password-less access for ansible account
    copy:
      src: ansible
      dest: /etc/sudoers.d/ansible
...
```

$ ansible-playbook -Kk -e user_name=$USER setup.yml

We have now fully documented the steps we ran through with ad hoc commands. Not only this; these commands are repeatable and correct as they are now recorded in the Playbook. From now on we can drop the password prompts, as we have ensured correct SSH key authentication and passwordless access to privilege escalation.

Summary

Wow, that is all the words that I have. Having created the *setup.yml* Playbook now, we could easily add new managed hosts without any concerns over their accurate inclusion in are managed hosts. Everything will be configured as it has been on the existing hosts. We concentrated on managing users in this chapter and having reached the end, apart from having created a truly awesome YAML Playbook, you have learned a whole heap.

Starting with the loop control in Ansible, we saw how we could manage more than one account with a single task, leading to the when clause that we could use to examine a variable to determine if the task should run or not. These variables could be facts from the system or passed to Ansible, as we used them. In creating users, we had to talk about passwords and password hashes. These are one-way encrypted files that cannot be decrypted. We demonstrated how authentication can work where passwords cannot be decrypted, and the **openssl** command was a useful tool used here.

We then transferred the ad hoc commands we used earlier to configure the managed devices into a Playbook, to document the setup and allow us to bring in new managed hosts easily without needing to remember each ad hoc command needed. This truly is a milestone for you, and the Playbook you have created will prove useful for you within your own projects.

CHAPTER 7

Working with Variables and Facts

We have already touched upon both variables and facts with previous examples that we have used and learned. In this chapter we can really consolidate that knowledge by investigating facts that can be collected or *gathered* on managed devices. That includes retrieving items such as the IP address, hostname, and fully qualified domain name. The previous are all facts that can be used as variables in the Playbook, either in clauses to control execution or as values to keys. We will extend the inventory variables we have used thus far, to allow for package and service name differences that occur with products such as the Apache HTTPD server. By the end of this chapter, you will have installed Apache on both CentOS and Ubuntu using a single task.

Gathering Facts

Facts are collected automatically by Playbooks unless disabled via the *gather_facts* key. It is the Ansible Python module *setup* that is executed to gather these facts. From the command, we can see system facts using ad hoc commands and the *setup* module. In the first example we display all facts before filtering the results in the second example.

Listing 7-1. Displaying Facts

```
$ ansible all -m setup
$ ansible all -m setup -a "filter='*_distribution_*'"
```

Filters work by using wildcards to represent character ranges in the same way as *file globbing* at the command line shell. This can be a useful alternative to piping the output to **grep** when the power of a full regular expression is not required.

Printing OS Information

Working within a Playbook, we could explicitly run the *setup* module, but as long as we have not disabled fact collection with **gather_facts: false**, we will be able to use each fact as a variable. We will now create a new project directory to work within to start looking at software upgrades across both CentOS and Ubuntu systems.

Listing 7-2. Creating New Ansible Project to Print OS Details

```
$ mkdir $HOME/ansible/upgrade ; cd $HOME/ansible/upgrade
$ ansible --version | grep 'config file'
  config file = /home/tux/.ansible.cfg
$ ansible-config dump --only-changed
DEFAULT_BECOME(/home/tux/.ansible.cfg) = True
DEFAULT_BECOME_METHOD(/home/tux/.ansible.cfg) = sudo
DEFAULT_HOST_LIST(/home/tux/.ansible.cfg) = ['/home/tux/
inventory']
DEFAULT_REMOTE_USER(/home/tux/.ansible.cfg) = ansible
$ vim upgrade.yml
---
- name: Upgrade Systems
  hosts: all
```

```
become: true
gather_facts: true
tasks:
  - name: Print Host Details
    debug:
      msg: "{{ item }}"
    loop:
      - "{{ ansible_hostname }}"
      - "{{ ansible_distribution }}"
      - "{{ ansible_distribution_version }}"
...
```
$ **ansible-playbook upgrade.yml**

Note We use the loop operator here, but you could also print the one message with all variables. For us, we can review the loop operator and reduce page width used by extra long lines. Later in the chapter, we will look at how we can fold long lines needed within keys.

Upgrading Systems

It just so happens that my CentOS 8 client system uses 8.0 rather than the currently available 8.2. I am sure this was just due to the ISO file that was used to install the client OS, but also indicates how easy it is to have out of date systems in your environment. We can and will make great use of these facts to control which systems are updated. In the following task, we only execute on the CentOS hosts that are not equal to 8.2. The *ansible_distribution_version* variable stores this as a text value, which we use in the comparison. Returning to the *upgrade.yml* Playbook, we can first remove the original task that printed the variables before adding the new task to run the package update. You are welcome to keep the first task if you so wish; we are open here at Apress. The first task is no longer required; however, the Playbook will still work if you prefer to add a new task and retain the original.

Tip   A **when** clause can grow quite long, as we can understand. By using the **fold** operator ❯, we are able to span multiple lines without affecting the clause itself. Don't forget to indent the folded lines to two spaces inside of the clause itself.

Listing 7-3. Updating CentOS Hosts

```
$ vim upgrade.yml
---
- name: Upgrade Systems
  hosts: all
  become: true
  gather_facts: true
  tasks:
    - name: Upgrade CentOS
      package:
        name: "*"
        state: latest
      when: >
        ansible_distribution == "CentOS" and
        ansible_distribution_version != "8.2"
...
$ ansible-playbook upgrade.yml
```

Running this Playbook for the first time will update the CentOS 8 client system. Running it a second time, no update will be required, as both systems will be at the correct and latest version.

To update the Ubuntu system, we can research the latest 18.04 release, which is currently *18.04.5*. We need to dig into the *ansible_lsb.descripton* variable to see this. The following ad hoc command illustrates the ansible_ lsb array, which is available by default on Ubuntu systems.

Listing 7-4. Decting the Full Ubuntu Version

```
$ ansible ubuntu -m setup -a "filter=ansible_lsb*"
172.16.120.188 | SUCCESS => {
    "ansible_facts": {
        "ansible_lsb": {
            "codename": "bionic",
            "description": "Ubuntu 18.04.5 LTS",
            "id": "Ubuntu",
            "major_release": "18",
            "release": "18.04"
        }
    },
    "changed": false
}
```

Note   If we needed the *ansible_lsb* array on the CentOS host, we would install the package *redhat-lsb-core*. We don't need this package, so we haven't installed it.

Adding both CentOS and Ubuntu condition groups to the existing *when* clause in the Playbook, we will have a single task that could update both sets of hosts. To control the processing of each set of conditions, we group related elements with parentheses and combine the two sets of bracketed condition groups with the logical OR operator. The edited Playbook follows for you to create and practice with.

Listing 7-5. Upgrading Both Ubuntu and CentOS in a Single Task

```
$ vim upgrade.yml
---
- name: Upgrade Systems
  hosts: all
  become: true
  gather_facts: true
  tasks:
    - name: Upgrade Older Systems
      package:
        name: "*"
        state: latest
      when: >
        (ansible_distribution == "CentOS" and
        ansible_distribution_version != "8.2") or
        (ansible_distribution == "Ubuntu" and
        ansible_lsb.description != "Ubuntu 18.04.5 LTS")
...
```

We have seen that variables can be read from the inventory, from the **-e** option, as well as facts from the systems; however, we can also define variables within the Playbook itself. These variables are especially useful to us in an example such as this. Defining the version numbers early in the Playbook makes it easy to view and edit as required when new versions are released. Take a look at the updated Playbook in the following example and I am sure you will get the idea.

Listing 7-6. Setting Variables Inside the Playbook

```
$ vim ugrade.yml
---
- name: Upgrade Systems
  hosts: all
  become: true
  gather_facts: true
  vars:
    - ubuntu_version: "Ubuntu 18.04.5 LTS"
    - centos_version: "8.2"
  tasks:
    - name: Upgrade Older Systems
      package:
        name: "*"
        state: latest
      when: >
        (ansible_distribution == "CentOS" and
        ansible_distribution_version != centos_version) or
        (ansible_distribution == "Ubuntu" and
        ansible_lsb.description != ubuntu_version)
...
```

Being able to check the current version set within the Playbook and update it easily at the top of the file is very convenient, helping document the enforced version as well as being super easy to edit. I would highly recommend executing the Playbook to check your own typing has been exemplary! The 4-hour exam flies by, and the quicker you are at writing accurate YAML, the better prepared you are for the exam.

Installing Apache

As we have seen, using the *package* module, rather than *yum* or *apt*, helps Ansible and our Playbooks maintain that all important *agnostic* attitude toward the OS, working across all supported platforms. However, we cannot cater for differences in the package name, and that is where inventory variables can race to our aid.

Important   Although the **package** module is very helpful, there is a cost for its simplicity. There are only a very few options to the **package** module, as it has to work across many different packagers. Using the underlying **apt** or **yum** module will provide you with more functionality while losing the agnostic nature of the generic module. It is important to understand the differences between the generic and specific module. A quick **ansible-doc** against the *package* and *yum* modules can help your understanding.

We will now create a new project to deploy the Apache web server. The package name is httpd on CentOS and apache2 on Ubuntu. First, let's update the inventory variables.

Listing 7-7. Updating the Ansible Inventory Variables to Support Apache Installation

```
$ echo "apache_pkg: httpd" >> ~/group_vars/centos
$ echo "apache_pkg: apache2" >> ~/group_vars/ubuntu
$ ansible-inventory --yaml --list
all:
  children:
    centos:
      hosts:
```

```
    172.16.120.161:
      admin_group: wheel
      ansible_connection: local
      apache_pkg: httpd
    172.16.120.185:
      admin_group: wheel
      apache_pkg: httpd
  ubuntu:
    children:
      bionic:
        hosts:
          172.16.120.188:
            admin_group: sudo
            ansible_python_interpreter: /usr/bin/python3
            apache_pkg: apache2
  ungrouped: {}
```

We may also choose to print the variables from a specific host; these will include those variables defined at both the host and group level. If we choose the controller, we will be able see this behavior, as it is currently the only system with host specific variables set as well as group variables.

Listing 7-8. Listing Variables Associated with a Specific Host

```
$ ansible-inventory --yaml --host 172.16.120.161
admin_group: wheel
ansible_connection: local
apache_pkg: httpd
```

Having set and confirmed the inventory variables, we are now able to move on with the new project to install Apache.

Listing 7-9. Creating the New Apache Project

```
$ mkdir $HOME/ansible/apache
$ cd $HOME/ansible/apache
$ vim simple_apache.yml
---
- name: Install Apache
  hosts: all
  become: true
  gather_facts: false
  tasks:
    - name:  Install Apache Package
      package:
        name: "{{ apache_pkg }}"
        state: present
...
$ ansible-playbook simple_apache.yml
TASK [Install Apache Package]
changed: [172.16.120.185]
changed: [172.16.120.161]
changed: [172.16.120.188]
```

With this simple single task, we were able to install Apache on the three systems. Having great planning combined with great software and great administrators, we are able to conquer the most formidable challenges placed before us. We also do need to remind ourselves that we have literally just installed the software and NOT configured the service. This will come as we start to work our way through the remaining chapters.

Summary

We are now masters of Ansible variables and facts. Having reached the end of this chapter, you should be pleased and proud with your progress. The *setup* module can be used to display facts from our managed devices. Using the *filter* argument to the module, we are able to drill to specific items we need to research. If **gather_facts** is enabled within a play, the setup module will automatically run, making the variables available to you.

Variables used outside of a *when* clause need to be double-quoted and inside double-brace brackets for good measure:

```
name: "{{ ansible_package }}"
```

Variables used with a when clause do not need quoting in the same way, but text strings do need to be quoted:

```
when: ansible_distribution == "CentOS"
```

These variables can come from many locations. This chapter used inventory variables, play variables, as well as facts. Having discovered these variables, we were able to see how useful they become in allowing flexible execution. Making use of *when* clauses allows conditional evaluation to determine if a task executes or not. We constructed a complex clause using both logical **OR** and logical **AND** operators. As the clause becomes longer, we used the fold operation, the **>**, to allow multiple indented lines in the clause.

We also used this module to review commands we have previously used and do not want to forget.

Listing 7-10. Commands Reviewed in This Chapter

```
$ ansible --version | grep "config file"
$ ansible-config dump --only-changed
$ ansible-inventory --list --yaml
$ ansible-inventory --host 172.16.120.161 --yaml
$ ansible ubuntu -m setup -a "filter=*lsb*"
```

CHAPTER 8

Working with Files and Templates

We have been able to deliver the *sudoers* files for the tux and ansible user accounts and we are well aware that files can be distributed with Ansible. Although this is good for some files, it may not be adequate for many other files. Where files contain many lines and options, we may prefer just to change the lines that we need and not the complete file. Delivering a complete file would provide a single monolithic solution, whereas we can meet a variety of needs by configuring the options that we need for each given scenario. In this chapter we investigate how we can copy complete files, dynamically create files with new content, edit files in place with the *lineinfile* module, and use Jinja 2 templates to create files meeting more complex needs.

The Copy Module

We have already used this module and it has delivered simple small files to the managed devices. This can be the complete file using the *src* arguments to the module or we can create dynamic content using the *content* argument.

© Andrew Mallett 2021
A. Mallett, *Red Hat Certified Engineer (RHCE) Study Guide*,
https://doi.org/10.1007/978-1-4842-6861-2_8

Using SRC

Having already seen the use of the *src* argument using the *sudoers* files, we will feel confident with it. Let's extend it just a little by delivering web content to the newly deployed web servers. As the Apache web service starts after the installation on Ubuntu, we can easily test the deployment on that host using **curl**. We will deliver to all hosts the web content that they need to promote our company to the world! Using **directory_mode: true** within the *copy* module, we allow the complete directory to be copied.

Listing 8-1. Copy Web Content from Controller to Managed Devices

```
$ cd $HOME/ansible/apache ; mkdir web
$ echo "Welcome" > web/index.html
$ echo "Peterborough, UK" > web/contact.html
$ ls web
contact.html   index.html
$ vim simple_apache.yml
---
- name: Install Apache
  hosts: all
  become: true
  gather_facts: false
  tasks:
    - name:  Install Apache Package
      package:
        name: "{{ apache_pkg }}"
        state: present
    - name: Copy web content
      copy:
        src: web/*
        directory_mode: true
```

```
      dest: /var/www/html
...
$ ansible-playbook simple_apache.yml
TASK [Copy web content]
changed: [172.16.120.161]
changed: [172.16.120.188]
changed: [172.16.120.185]
$ curl 172.16.120.188 #use ip of ubuntu host
Welcome
```

Content Is King

Where a file's content is quite simple and, most likely short, we can create it dynamically using the *content* argument to the *copy* module. To demonstrate this, we will create a new project for the */etc/motd* file. This is the text file that is used as the message of the day when you log in to the system. Nobody ever reads this message, but we feel compelled to create a message for our users. I don't know why; it is just one of those SysAdmin things.

Listing 8-2. Delivering the MOTD File with Ansible

```
$ mkdir $HOME/ansible/motd ; cd $HOME/ansible/motd
$ vim motd.yml
---
- name: Manage the /etc/motd file
  become: true
  hosts: all
  gather_facts: true
  tasks:
    - name: Copy /etc/motd
      copy:
        dest: /etc/motd
```

```
    content: |
        This system is managed by Ansible
        The system name is {{ ansible_hostname }}
        The IP address is {{ ansible_default_ipv4.address }}
...
$ ansible-playbook motd.yml
$ ssh ansible@<ubuntu ip> #login via ssh to the ubuntu or
client system
This system is managed by Ansible
The system name is ubuntu
The IP address is 172.16.120.188
Last login: Wed Nov 25 14:16:09 2020 from 172.16.120.161
$ exit #to return to controller
```

Differing Fold Operators

In the *motd.yml* we used the fold operator as **|**, the vertical bar. Previously, we had used the fold operator as **>**, the greater than symbol. So why have two and what is the difference? Well, those are great questions, which I will try to answer here.

- **>** : We used this in the **when** clause where we needed a single line, even though we had extended across many lines. Using the **>** operator, newlines are replaced with spaces.

- **|** : We have just used this in the *motd.yml* in the content argument. We want the content to be on multiple lines and the **|** operator maintains the newlines in the folded string.

Editing Files in Place

There will be many files where we want to implement or replace an existing setting for a file that already exists on the managed device. We could replace the complete file but that may not be required or necessarily be desired. It is very easy to imagine two Ansible projects needing to edit the same configuration file and causing conflicts. Changing only the lines that we want allows for the coexistence of projects that need to configure their own independent lines within the same file. As well as avoiding these configuration collisions, we use less bandwidth in delivering the changes.

Working within a new project for the SSH server, we will ensure that the root user is not permitted to log in via the service. We already know that SSH must be configured on managed devices, as we use SSH to connect to the remote systems. First, we will compare the SSHD configuration differences that exist between CentOS and Ubuntu. We manage this using an ad hoc command to search for the desired setting from the *sshd_config*.

Listing 8-3. Searching Current SSHD Settings, Annotate the Output with the OS of the Given System

```
$ ansible all -m shell -a "grep PermitRootLogin /etc/ssh/
  sshd_config"
(CentOS)172.16.120.161 | CHANGED | rc=0 >>
PermitRootLogin yes
# the setting of "PermitRootLogin without-password".
(CentOS)172.16.120.185 | CHANGED | rc=0 >>
PermitRootLogin yes
# the setting of "PermitRootLogin without-password".
(Ubuntu)172.16.120.188 | CHANGED | rc=0 >>
#PermitRootLogin prohibit-password
# the setting of "PermitRootLogin without-password".
```

117

Reviewing (posh word for reading) the output, we can see that the setting is active in CentOS and allows root login. In Ubuntu, the setting is not active, but the default setting allows root login only when not using password-based authentication. We want a consistent setting maintained on all systems that prevents root login via SSH. It is not required that we have direct access to the root account via SSH and it is certainly not secure, especially for public facing systems. The *lineinfile* module will do the exact job we need to edit this file.

Listing 8-4. Editing the SSHD Configuration

```
$ mkdir $HOME/ansible/ssh ; cd $HOME/ansible/ssh
$ vim sshd.yml
---
- name: Manage SSHD
  hosts: all
  gather_facts: false
  become: true
  tasks:
    - name: Edit SSHD Config
      lineinfile:
        path: /etc/ssh/sshd_config
        regexp: '^PermitRootLogin '
        insertafter: '#PermitRootLogin'
        line: 'PermitRootLogin no'
...
$ ansible-playbook sshd.yml
TASK [Edit SSHD Config] changed: [172.16.120.161]
changed: [172.16.120.188]
changed: [172.16.120.185]
$ ansible all -m shell -a "grep PermitRootLogin /etc/ssh/
  sshd_config"
```

```
172.16.120.161 | CHANGED | rc=0 >>
PermitRootLogin no
# the setting of "PermitRootLogin without-password".
172.16.120.188 | CHANGED | rc=0 >>
#PermitRootLogin prohibit-password
PermitRootLogin no
# the setting of "PermitRootLogin without-password".
172.16.120.185 | CHANGED | rc=0 >>
PermitRootLogin no
# the setting of "PermitRootLogin without-password"
```

Important We have edited the file, but we have not restarted the service, meaning the setting is not effective yet. We will modify the Playbook in the next chapter to restart the service on a file change.

The *lineinfile* module is very powerful, so let me step you through the arguments used to help you understand:

- *path*: This is the simple one, the path on the managed device of the file to edit.

- *regexp*: If the line is likely to exist, we can search for it, allowing replacement the current line.

- *insertafter*: If the line does not exist, a new line will be added to the end of the file or after the line that we specify here. We will add the line, if required, after the commented line.

- *line*: This is the line that we dictate *must* be in the file and the desired setting we want to implement.

Using Templates

We have seen with the message of the day (MOTD) file that we created earlier, that it is most certainly possible to pass facts and variables into a file using the *content* argument to the *copy* module. Perhaps it did work for us as, I think, we used just two variables. As the needs and complexity of the file increases, we may find Jinja 2 templates much more convenient. We will move back into the *$HOME/ansible/motd* directory to develop this further, initially creating the template to house the text and variables.

Listing 8-5. Building a Jinja 2 Template

```
$ cd $HOME/ansible/motd
$ vim motd.j2
Welcome to {{ ansible_hostname }}
The system uses:
{{ ansible_distribution }} {{ ansible_distribution_version }}
The IP Address is: {{ ansible_default_ipv4.address }}
```

The template is a much more convenient method for larger files, as the variables can be placed inside of the template for ease of layout. This is great for keeping your Playbook uncluttered and the template the focus for the variables. Rather than using the *copy* module, we use the *template* module to ensure the variables are rendered correctly at runtime.

Listing 8-6. Using the Template Module in Playbooks

```
$ vim motd.yml
---
- name: Manage the /etc/motd file
  become: true
  hosts: all
  gather_facts: true
  tasks:
```

```
  - name: Copy /etc/motd
    template:
      dest: /etc/motd
      src: motd.j2
...
$ ansible-playbook motd.yml
$ ssh ansible@172.16.120.185
Welcome to client
The system uses:
CentOS 8.2
The IP Address is: 172.16.120.185
Last login: Thu Nov 26 12:10:05 2020 from 172.16.120.161
$ exit
```

Placing variables and text, including possible configuration items, in templates will allow for a much more complex projects where setting values can be populated from variables.

Summary

In this chapter it was our goal to become Zen Masters of distributing files and templates within Ansible. How do you feel, and did I help you attain the goal?

Let's just take a little time to allow all of our emotions to settle and recount just some of our journey. Start with the five Ansible modules used in this chapter:

- **copy**

- **template**

- **lineinfile**

- **shell**

- **package**

Sure, we had seen the *package* module before, but this time we saw that the agnostic nature of the module only stretched so far. We needed to set the inventory variable to assign the correct package name. We had also used the *copy* module previously; this time, though, we looked at the *content* argument rather than the *src* argument that we used before. Using *content* allows for the file's content to be defined dynamically within the Playbook itself. That also means we can render variables that we could use as we initially did within the MOTD file. It was here we also learned of the two *fold* operators, | and >, the former supporting the retention of line feeds and the latter changing them to spaces.

Perhaps the king of the modules in the chapter, though, is the *lineinfile* module, allowing us to edit or add individual lines to a file rather than replacing it in a wholesale manner. Some, though, would undoubtedly vote for the *template* module, which extends the capabilities of *copy/content* but storing the variables and text in a Jinja 2 template file. What was your most useful feature of this chapter? Do let us know.

CHAPTER 9

Managing Services Using Ansible

As an amazing system administrator, you need to be able to face the differences in Linux distributions and face them with a smile. We have just installed the Apache web server; on CentOS the associated service did not start after the installation, whereas it did in Ubuntu. Of course, ultimately, we would like the service running on all web servers, regardless of the distribution. Not only are we faced with this issue relating to services; we have edited the SSHD configuration on all systems using the *lineinfile* module, but those changes are not affected until a restart of the service itself. So, our systems are still at risk. In this chapter we will solve some of these issues and prepare for future solutions by implementing both the *service* and *systemd* module in Ansible. We will see how we can start and enable services as needed, as well as stopping and disabling services we do not need. Critically, for changes in configuration files that affect services, we can restart the service on a change in the file's state. This is a new element to us in Ansible, known as a **handler**.

© Andrew Mallett 2021
A. Mallett, *Red Hat Certified Engineer (RHCE) Study Guide*,
https://doi.org/10.1007/978-1-4842-6861-2_9

The Service Module

In very much the same vein as the *package* module, the generic service
module can help you manage services without care for the underlying
OS. In just the same manner, this equally helps and hinders us. It is useful
because of the module's agonistic nature; however, it cannot help with the
specific features of an underlying service manager. The documentation,
ansible-doc service, will print the help on the module and illustrate the
sparse arguments supported. It has the basics, though, and most times we
can make do with this module.

The Systemd Module

Both Ubuntu 18.04 and CentOS 8 use the more recent *systemd* service
manager. If we are uncertain of the manager, then Ansible can help us
discover the underlying service manager on any given host. This is supplied
as an Ansible fact waiting to be interrogated by us at any time, as can the
software package manager. Let's investigate this on all of our systems using
ad hoc commands.

Listing 9-1. Interrogating Ansible Facts to Determine Managers

```
$ ansible all -m setup -a "filter=ansible_*_mgr"
172.16.120.188 | SUCCESS => {
    "ansible_facts": {
        "ansible_pkg_mgr": "apt",
        "ansible_service_mgr": "systemd"
    },
    "changed": false
}
172.16.120.161 | SUCCESS => {
    "ansible_facts": {
```

```
        "ansible_pkg_mgr": "dnf",
        "ansible_service_mgr": "systemd",
        "discovered_interpreter_python": "/usr/libexec/
        platform-python"
    },
    "changed": false
}
172.16.120.185 | SUCCESS => {
    "ansible_facts": {
        "ansible_pkg_mgr": "dnf",
        "ansible_service_mgr": "systemd",
        "discovered_interpreter_python": "/usr/libexec/
        platform-python"
    },
    "changed": false
}
```

We can see that all of the systems use *systemd* as the underlying
manager for services and can be viewed in the fact: **ansible_service_mgr**.
The differences we see are contained in the **ansible_pkg_mgr**, where
Ubuntu uses *apt* and CentOS makes use of *dnf*. Using the *systemd* module,
we make available many more features such as masking and unmasking
services that are not available with the *service* module. Mainly we can
stick with the agnostic and generic *service* module; after all, what else do
we want to do with a service other than enable/disable it or start/stop it?
Ninety percent of the time the *service* module is enough. For our Sunday
best and the odd occasion that we need to mask or unmask a service, we
reserve the *systemd* module.

Using Ansible Handlers

Handlers are a similar dictionary list within a play to the tasks dictionary. As the names suggest, they contain a list of handlers rather than tasks. Simple, really; it is all in the name. A handler, unlike a task, is executed only when notified by some other task. Many tasks can notify exactly the same handler, but the handler will only execute once. If there are no tasks that notify the handler, then it is not executed. Returning to our SSH project, we can have the SSHD service restart on changes to the configuration file. We will do this by implementing our first ever handler. Although we know the SSH service must be running for use to communicate with Ansible, we can also implement a task to ensure the service is both *enabled* and *started*. By enabled, we mean the service should start automatically upon system boot.

Listing 9-2. Managing Services and Implementing Handlers

```
$ cd $HOME/ansible/ssh
$ vim sshd.yml
PLAY RECAP *************************************************
***********************************************************
*
---
- name: Manage SSHD
  hosts: all
  gather_facts: false
  become: true
  tasks:
    - name: Ensure SSHD Started and Enabled
      service:
        name: sshd
        enabled: true
        state: started
```

```
  - name: Edit SSHD Config
    lineinfile:
      path: /etc/ssh/sshd_config
      regexp: '^PermitRootLogin '
      insertafter: '#PermitRootLogin'
      line: 'PermitRootLogin no '
    notify: restart_sshd
  handlers:
  - name: restart_sshd
    service:
      name: sshd
      state: restarted
......
$ ansible-playbook sshd.yml
TASK [Edit SSHD Config]
changed: [172.16.120.161]
changed: [172.16.120.188]
changed: [172.16.120.185]

RUNNING HANDLER [restart_sshd]
changed: [172.16.120.161]
changed: [172.16.120.188]
changed: [172.16.120.185]
```

Important   Please take note that we added a space after the word *no* in the *line* argument to the *lineinfile* module. To notify the handler the configuration file must change, adding a space changes the file without any impact to the actual configuration.

Ensure SSHD Started and Enabled

This first task is not required to implement handlers; please do not think that we must have a task to enable the service for the handler to operate. It is likely though, that if we need to restart a service via a handler, we will also have a task that ensures that the service is enabled and started. Other possible states for both the *service* and *systemd* module include *reloaded*, *restarted*, *started*, and *stopped*.

Edit SSHD Config

This is the task that checks for the presence of the required configuration line using the *lineinfile* module. You will notice that we have added an argument to the task, meaning at the same indentation level as the name of the task and the module name. The **notify argument** is used to link this task to the named handler. The name we supply must exactly match the name of the handler. To help with this, I always name my handlers in lowercase and use the underscore to join words in place of spaces. This is probably a good naming standard for both tasks and handlers.

The Handler: restart_sshd

Finally, we have the handler as a list item within the handlers dictionary to the play. We use the same *service* module referencing the SSHD service. The state, though, is set to *restarted*. Using either of the states, *restarted* or *reloaded* (rereads configuration if supported by service), within an Ansible task would mean that the task would always execute. Having it in an Ansible handler allows us to execute the module only when required. This is pure magic and a feature for you to enjoy and take further.

Handlers Do Not Run when They Are Not Notified

Running the Playbook again, for a second time, we will observe that the handler does not execute. As there is no need to change the configuration, the notify option is not called and the handlers sit peacefully, catching up on some well-deserved rest and recuperation. From the output of the Playbook, there is no reference to the handler in any way, shape, or form.

Listing 9-3. When the Handler Is Not Called, There Is No Reference to It Within the Playbook Output

```
$ ansible-playbook sshd.yml
PLAY [Manage SSHD]
TASK [Ensure SSHD Started and Enabled]
ok: [172.16.120.161]
ok: [172.16.120.188]
ok: [172.16.120.185]
TASK [Edit SSHD Config]
ok: [172.16.120.161]
ok: [172.16.120.188]
ok: [172.16.120.185]
```

Service Facts

We can gain a list of services that are present on any given system by collecting them as facts. This lists all services on the system and is independent of their current state. The *setup* module gathers our standard facts collection; for a list of services we need to execute the *service_facts* module as an independent task. This can be collected independently of the *setup* module and without reference to the status of *gather_facts*. This becomes useful to us by allowing control of the execution of subsequent tasks based on the presence or absence of a service. For example, if we want to run the Apache web service we may want to first check that the Nginx web service is masked, so unable to be started. For us, we already know that the Apache web service has started without issues, but we cannot be certain of this in a larger environment. We can assume that mainly the Nginx service will not be present, which means that there is no point just having a task to mask the Nginx service unit. If we took this approach, the Playbook would error on that task if the service is not present. We need the *service_facts* module and the skill in constructing a little logic to smooth any potential issues, to make us the Ansible gurus we have always aimed to be.

Let's return to the *$HOME/ansible/apache* project directory where we can create a new Playbook to explicitly check for and mask the Nginx service. The task should only run if the Nginx service is present on the system and does not depend on the current state of that service. We are the final authority in managing our systems, so let us prove this now!

Listing 9-4. Masking a Service If It Is Present on the System

```
$ cd $HOME/ansible/apache
$ vim nginx.yml
---
- name: Manage masking of NGINX
  hosts: all
  become: true
  gather_facts: false
  tasks:
    - name: Collect service list
      service_facts:
    - name: Mask Nginx
      systemd:
        name: nginx
        masked: true
```

```
      state: stopped
    when: "'nginx.service' in ansible_facts.services"
...
```

$ **ansible-playbook nginx.yml**

The *when* clause now requires that we begin strings with double-quotes, as we did not start the clause with a variable. The service name is single-quoted to set it apart. The *service* array, created by the *service_facts* module, will contain a list of services on the system. We simply need to look for *nginx.service* within the array to determine its presence on the system. Currently, on all three of our systems, we do not have the Nginx service, so the task does not need to run.

If we wanted to test the logic that we are using here, we could add another task that simply prints text to the console, but only on the Ubuntu system as we now look for the Apache2 service.

Listing 9-5. Testing Service Logic

$ **vim nginx.yml**

```
---
- name: Manage masking of NGINX
  hosts: all
  become: true
  gather_facts: false
  tasks:
    - name: Collect service list
      service_facts:
    - name: Mask Nginx
      systemd:
        name: nginx
        masked: true
        state: stopped
      when: "'nginx.service' in ansible_facts.services"
```

```
  - name: Is Apache service
    debug:
      msg: "This must be Ubuntu!"
    when: "'apache2.service' in ansible_facts.services"
...
```

```
$ ansible-playbook nginx.yml
TASK [Is Apache service]
skipping: [172.16.120.161]
skipping: [172.16.120.185]
ok: [172.16.120.188] => {
    "msg": "This must be Ubuntu!"
}
```

Summary

Would you believe it? The four horsemen of the Apocalypse now bend their knees to your superiority and mastery of Ansible. Your use of logic to control task execution has surpassed anything that you could have imagined when starting this book. Not only this, you have been able to choose to restart services but, crucially, only when needed. This is some form of AI or artificial intelligence that you have added to your Playbooks, which have become majestic. Your name now is only ever mentioned in hushed tones and always with absolute reverence.

Within our Playbooks we became used to and familiar with the *service* and *systemd* modules. These can be used to control services with a generic module and a specific module for systemd used on most modern Linux distributions. I would suggest erring toward the generic module, so we avoid errors with non-Linux OSs and older Linux systems such as CentOS 6: systems that do not implement systemd. We should reserve the use of the specialized *systemd* module to those special times when we need access to the specifics that it provisions.

We learned to master the use of handlers within our carefully crafted Playbooks. Using handlers, we can ensure that they are only executed when called by another task. In this way we were able to ensure that an edited SSHD configuration file notifies the handler used to restart the SSHD service. We created a highly tuned and perfect Playbook to manage the SSH service on our managed devices.

We did not stop here, no, not by a long way. We want you to be the reference for Ansible within your organization, the go-to person who can fix anything Ansible related. To this goal, we extended Ansible standard facts by using the *service_facts* module. This created an array or list of services on the system, allowing us to create the required logic to run tasks related to services. For us, this meant that we could ensure that only one web service was ever to be loaded on the device, ensuring that the Nginx web service was masked or prevented from starting where we needed Apache to run. Pure genius! That is what I have heard as people walk reverently past your door now; pure genius! Bask in that glory before moving on to encrypting sensitive data with Ansible Vault, which we cover next.

CHAPTER 10

Securing Sensitive Data with Ansible Vault

Some data that we need to use within our Playbooks may contain data that is sensitive and needs to be secured in some way, shape, or form. Rather than storing this sensitive data in cleartext directly in the Playbook, we can use **ansible-vault** to create a *cyphertext* file that we use with the Playbook. A simple requirement for this would be the *user.yml* file that we created earlier in the *$HOME/ansible/setup* directory; the user's password is stored in the Playbook in cleartext, which is not exactly ideal. By using a variable for the password, we can include reference to an encrypted variables file to secure the Playbook operation, allowing us to rest more peacefully at night.

© Andrew Mallett 2021
A. Mallett, *Red Hat Certified Engineer (RHCE) Study Guide*,
https://doi.org/10.1007/978-1-4842-6861-2_10

Creating an External Variables File

Even if there is no need for encryption, we can still make use of part of the process by referencing an external file where variables are stored. Within an Ansible play, we already know that we can reference a list of variables. We saw using variables had become a very convenient way in which we could set version numbers used when deciding if we needed to update the distribution or not. If the list of variables is lengthy or is likely to become so, we may prefer to reference a file. It is most easy to implement this instead of using the dictionary **vars:** we use a dedicated task and module **include_vars**. Now, if we recall, within the *$HOME/ansible/upgrade/upgrade.yml* we made reference to just two variables, so it's hardly a lengthy list! But if you would be so kind as to humor me, we can quickly look at how we would reference an external file. There is no need to encrypt these variables, so we keep the variables stored as clear text YAML to begin with.

Listing 10-1. Storing Variables in an External YAML File

```
$ cd $HOME/ansible/upgrade ; cat upgrade.yml
---
- name: Upgrade Systems
  hosts: all
  become: true
  gather_facts: true
  vars:
    - ubuntu_version: "Ubuntu 18.04.5 LTS"
    - centos_version: "8.2"
  tasks:
    - name: Upgrade Older Systems
      package:
        name: "*"
        state: latest
```

```
      when: >
        (ansible_distribution == "CentOS" and
        ansible_distribution_version != centos_version) or
        (ansible_distribution == "Ubuntu" and
        ansible_lsb.description != ubuntu_version)
...
$ #we change the embedded variables to external variables
$ echo 'ubuntu_version: "Ubuntu 18.04.5 LTS"' >> version.yml
$ echo 'centos_version: "8.2"' >> version.yml
$ cat version.yml
ubuntu_version: "Ubuntu 18.04.5 LTS"
centos_version: "8.2"
$ vim upgrade .yml
---

- name: Upgrade Systems
  hosts: all
  become: true
  gather_facts: true
  tasks:
    - name: read the variables file
      include_vars:
        file: version.yml
    - name: Upgrade Older Systems
      package:
        name: "*"
        state: latest
      when: >
        (ansible_distribution == "CentOS" and
        ansible_distribution_version != centos_version) or
        (ansible_distribution == "Ubuntu" and
        ansible_lsb.description != ubuntu_version)

...
```

Encrypt Existing YAML File

When we need a more secure variable data store, we can simply encrypt the existing file. If the file does not exist, we can create a brand new file that is encrypted from the start. As we are starting with an existing YAML variable store, we will encrypt that existing file before we move on to creating a new encrypted file.

Listing 10-2. Encrypting an Existing YAML File

```
$ ansible-vault encrypt version.yml
New Vault password:
Confirm New Vault password:
Encryption successful
$ cat version.yml
$ANSIBLE_VAULT;1.1;AES256
37313034613630313333838303630383439326138323962333353837303862613
33166316163393263
63303563337373032646163626331643530346635663030650a3737343264333
33566383039366662
61323436383637663139393539646530383964336161613133656635303239
63064373166333735
62656139356237362a656364333134383039353333564356236362333438
3036633330336439
65306566631343364306139656561613830653137346533646136643832363030
43537363038393934
63333135303737613433623439636664323363383765303830626326565653
23433363033646335
35373361353736353166313036063062333266
$ ansible-vault view version.yml
Vault password:
ubuntu_version: "Ubuntu 18.04.5 LTS"
centos_version: "8.2"
```

Having encrypted the file, it has been protected by AES256 bit encryption, and a password needs to be entered to access the contents. The *view* subcommand can be used to see the contents in cleartext, and we could use the *edit* subcommand to allow editing of the file after the password is entered. To execute the Playbook referencing this file, we also need to supply the password.

Listing 10-3. Executing the Playbook When Variables Are Encrypted

```
$ ansible-playbook --ask-vault-pass upgrade.yml
Vault password:
```

The Playbook can now execute correctly, as the variables are available to the **ansible-playbook** command.

Creating New Encrypted Files

If the encrypted variables do not exist in a YAML file, we can create a new file directly with **ansible-vault**. On CentOS the default editor is **vim**. If we want the **ansible-vault** to open with **nano** or another editor, we can work with the *EDITOR* environment variable. Returning to the *setup* directory we can create an encrypted file for the user password variable.

Listing 10-4. Creating a New Encrypted YAML File Bypassing the Default Editor

```
$ cd $HOME/ansible/setup
$ EDITOR=nano ansible-vault create private.yml
New Vault password:
Confirm New Vault password (nano will then open)

user_password: Password1
```

```
$ $ ansible-vault view private.yml
Vault password:
user_password: Password1
```

Having created the new file, we can edit it at any stage using **ansible-vault edit private.yml**. Of course, we will need to enter the password used to encrypt the file. We won't need to edit the file, but in the real world this could well be required.

Note   Take great care with the password! Forgetting the password used will mean that access is lost to that file. NO! Storing on a Post-it note is not an option!

To make use of this, just as before, we will need to add the additional task to the Playbook. This time we are working with the *user.yml* that we created in the *$HOME/ansible/setup directory*.

Listing 10-5. Editing the user.yml

```
$ vim user.yml
---
- name: Manage User Account
  hosts: all
  become: true
  gather_facts: false
  tasks:
    - name: Read password variable
      include_vars:
        file: private.yml
    - name: Create User
      user:
        name: "{{ user_name }}"
```

```
      shell: /bin/bash
      state: present
      password: "{{ user_password | password_hash('sha512') }}"
      update_password: on_create
    when: user_create == 'yes'
  - name: Delete User
    user:
      name: "{{ user_name }}"
      state: absent
      remove:  true
    when: user_create == 'no'
...
$ ansible-playbook -e user_name=april -e user_create=yes \
  --ask-vault-pass user.yml
Vault password:
```

Read Vault Password

If the interactive method of entering the vault password is not possible, such as when scheduling a Playbook execution, it is possible to read the password from a file. I am not a big fan of this method though. To me, it is a little like the children's song, *"There's a hole in my bucket."* We are back at square one, having sensitive data in a cleartext file, but this time we store the vault password in cleartext. If we are forced to use this as a solution, then we certainly should ramp up the file security. In the example, we set the file to be read-only to the file's owner, using the module of **400**.

Listing 10-6. Reading the Vault Password from a File

```
$ echo Password1 > passwd.txt
$ chmod 400 passwd.txt
$ ansible-playbook -e user_name=may \
  -e user_create=yes --vault-password-file=passwd.txt user.yml
```

Summary

Protecting sensitive data, such as user passwords, should make an everyday presence in your Ansible world. You can become the triple-headed Cerberos and sit guarding your own gates of Hades. Humor put to one side, this is a serious matter. If any unauthorized access to a Playbook holding sensitive data—or the key to data such as a password—is gained, the data protection regulators within your geography are likely to jump on you like a ton of bricks. This is no longer an internal error, and it becomes reportable. Encrypting passwords and those default passwords used for Playbooks does allow you a level of protection while still automating your administration.

The command **ansible-vault** manages the encryption and decryption using the AES256 crypt algorithm. We can create new encrypted files or encrypt existing files. If necessary, we can remove the encryption altogether using the decrypt subcommand. This returns the file to cleartext. Should you ever feel that the encryption password has been compromised, you have the option with the re-key subcommand to specify a new key and reencrypt the file.

To access the encrypted file from a Playbook, we need to use the *--ask-vault-pass* option. Within the Ansible play where the variables are required, we must use the task module *include_vars* so we can reference the variable file. That variable file can be encrypted or unencrypted. Just because we want to include a variables file, it does not mean that it needs to be encrypted. Where access to many variables is required, a file may be the best solution.

## CHAPTER 11

Implementing a Full Apache Deployment

With great thanks to the amazing Douglas Adams and *"The Hitchhiker's Guide to the Galaxy,"* we all know that 42 is the ultimate answer—being the meaning of life, the universe, and everything. I would respectfully suggest that it may now be Ansible, and in this chapter I hope to persuade you with a demonstration of how much we can achieve using automation. We have used many of the tools and elements of Ansible that we need to know, meaning that we can start on something more powerful. We will work out everything that we need to do when installing Apache and have Ansible automate it on both Ubuntu and CentOS Linux distributions.

Deploying Apache

As I have just mentioned, a deployment of the Apache web server is not just a single task of installing the package. There are many smaller tasks that form together to make an awesome configuration where nothing is ever forgotten. When we look at pretty much the bare minimum in the deployment, we will need to include the following as tasks:

- Deploy the correct Apache package
- Start service, especially when we are working with Red Hat distributions; Debian-based systems usually start their services in the install

© Andrew Mallett 2021
A. Mallett, *Red Hat Certified Engineer (RHCE) Study Guide*,
https://doi.org/10.1007/978-1-4842-6861-2_11

- Open the correct port in the firewall manager: ufw for Ubuntu and firewalld for CentOS

- Make configuration changes to the distribution-specific Apache configuration files

- Use handlers to restart service on configuration change

- Deploy standard web content

- Configure DocumentRoot filesystem security

These represent the minimum tasks that we are likely to configure; of course it could be more, but just think for a moment how useful this will be. Once you have the list of tasks that you need, you can document the setup in the Playbook and automate that same configuration.

As we work through this chapter, we will learn new Ansible modules as well as recapping on previous modules we have learned. As always, we will ensure that we can repeatedly and correctly deploy the web service every time. We will be working with a single Playbook containing all tasks and handlers. Later we will see how using roles can streamline the Playbook. Rather than repeating the tasks in each and every Playbook where they are needed, roles store shared code that can be used in many Playbooks.

As we work through this chapter, the Playbook will grow to many lines. Rather than showing the complete Playbook file after each edit, we will list just the recent edits for each section. The complete Playbook will be listed at the chapter end. Your learning and understanding is my primary goal, and I want to make each learning step clear to you, which is why tasks are listed individually. To understand the big picture, the final completed Playbook helps you see what the final YAML should look like.

Apache Playbook

We will move into the *$HOME/ansible/apache* directory. Within this directory we have already created the Playbook, which has been used to deploy the web server and web content. We will start with this file and improve it as we work through the chapter. I will make a copy of the existing YAML Playbook before adjusting the new content.

Listing 11-1. Beginning a Full Apache Deployment

```
$ cd $HOME/ansible/apache
$ cp simple_apache.yml full_apache.yml
$ vim full_apache.yml
---
- name: Manage Apache Deployment
  hosts: all
  become: true
  gather_facts: true
  tasks:
    - name:  Install Apache Package
      package:
        name: "{{ apache_pkg }}"
        state: present
    - name: Copy web content
      copy:
        src: web/
        directory_mode: true
        dest: /var/www/html
    - name: Start and Enable Apache Service
      service:
```

```
    name: "{{ apache_pkg }}"
    state: started
    enabled: true
...
$ ansible-playbook full_apache.yml
```

Having created the new Playbook, we have made a couple of minor changes. We have changed the Play title to better suit the tasks we use, and we have started to collect Ansible facts, which we will use shortly. The new task we have added ensures that the Apache service is enabled and started. The service name conveniently matches the package name, so we are able to make use of the existing variable.

Dedicated Server Page

We should dedicate some time to templating practice. We can create a new template within the Apache project directory to deploy to our systems along with the other web content. The template will reside on the controller but not in the *web* directory we previously created, and it is copied using the *copy* module; we need the *template* module to serve Jinja 2 templates. The *template* module populates the variable content that we add to the template file.

Listing 11-2. Deploying a Jinja 2 Template as the server.html Web Page

```
$ vim server.j2
This is {{ ansible_hostname }}
We are running {{ ansible_distribution }}
$ vim full_apache.yml
    - name: Custom web content
      template:
        src: server.j2
        dest: /var/www/html/server.html
```

Note   I would recommend testing the Playbook at each stage, making it easier to detect and correct typos as they occur rather than more complex debugging when all changes have been added.

All About Firewalls

We can test access to the remote systems now. In a previous chapter I was able to demonstrate access to the Ubuntu system. This worked fine, as the service had started automatically and by default the firewall was not enabled in Ubuntu. Having now added the custom page and ensured the service will be running on all systems, we can test a little further. From the controller we should be able to access the controller's web service and that of Ubuntu, but most likely the firewall will block access on the CentOS client. The following lists the IP addresses used in my lab for each system:

- **172.16.120.161**: My CentOS controller

- **172.16.120.185**: My CentOS client

- **172.16.120.188**: My Ubuntu host

Listing 11-3. Testing HTTP Access to the Web Servers

```
$ curl 172.16.120.161/server.html
This is controller
We are running CentOS
$ curl 172.16.120.188/server.html
This is ubuntu
We are running Ubuntu
$ curl 172.16.120.185/server.html
curl: (7) Failed to connect to 172.16.120.185 port 80: No route
    to host
```

It would appear that we cannot connect to the client system but, with a little knowledge of CentOS, we should know that the *Firewalld* firewall is active by default. We do gain access on the controller and that too is CentOS, but remember we are accessing it from the controller and not remotely. When using Ansible to remedy the situation, we have the choice to disable the firewall on each system or enable the firewall on each system. The main target is consistency across all systems, but security also has to be prominent in this cyber-aware world. Bearing security in mind, we will choose to enable the firewall on each system; on Ubuntu *UFW* is used but disabled and on CentOS *Firewalld* is used and enabled. To start, we will add variables to identify the underlying firewall manager.

Listing 11-4. Updating Inventory Variables

```
$ echo "firewall_pkg: firewalld" >> $HOME/group_vars/centos
$ echo "firewall_pkg: ufw" >> $HOME/group_vars/ubuntu
$ ansible-inventory --yaml --host 172.16.120.161
admin_group: wheel
ansible_connection: local
apache_pkg: httpd
firewall_pkg: firewalld
$ ansible-inventory --yaml --host 172.16.120.188
admin_group: sudo
ansible_python_interpreter: /usr/bin/python3
apache_pkg: apache2
firewall_pkg: ufw
```

Now that we have the variables configured, we can configure the firewalls on our systems. We will ensure the correct firewall package is installed and the service is running. This is where we can use the *firewall_pkg* variable for both the package name and service name. Then, using the correct module to manage the installed firewall, we enable SSH and HTTP. This is a great revision for the *when* clause also.

Listing 11-5. Enabling the Ubuntu UFW Firewall and Allowing
Access to SSH and HTTP

```
$ vim full_apache.yml
    - name: Firewall Package
      package:
        name: "{{ firewall_pkg }}"
        state: present
    - name: Firewall Service
      service:
        name: "{{ firewall_pkg }}"
        enabled: true
        state: started
    - name: UFW Ubuntu
      ufw:
          state: enabled
          policy: deny
          rule: allow
          port: "{{ item }}"
          proto: tcp
      loop:
        - "80"
        - "22"
      when: ansible_distribution == "Ubuntu"
    - name: Firewalld CentOS
      firewalld:
        service: "{{ item }}"
        permanent: true
        immediate: true
        state: enabled
      loop:
        - "http"
        - "ssh"
      when: ansible_distribution == "CentOS"
```

We have written all of these firewall-related tasks in one go. What we don't want to do is enable the firewall service and find out that SSH or TCP port 22 is not enabled in the default settings for the firewall system. That would lock us and Ansible out of the system. We do usually advocate testing tasks as we create them; but we also need to be aware of possible pitfalls in our methodology.

We introduce the *ufw* and *firewalld* Ansible modules:

- **firewalld**: Here, we use the *permanent* and *immediate* arguments. Firewalld can implement the *permanent* settings by writing to the back-end configuration files. These settings are not loaded until the service is restarted, and this is why we also have the *immediate* argument to assign the settings to the runtime configuration.

- **ufw**: The UFW firewall service can be started, but the configuration can be independently disabled. This was the default on my Ubuntu system. Within the module we first *enable* the firewall. We then set the default *policy* to *deny*. Any packet that does not match an existing rule will have the default policy applied. This means that we need to explicitly allow the incoming traffic that we want to succeed.

The Apache Configuration File

The Apache directive *ServerName* used in its configuration is not set by default and will cause warning in the log files. We can easily resolve this annoyance by setting the directive with the systems hostname. The hostname is available through an ansible fact. The location and name of the Apache configuration files differ, as you may have already guessed, between Ubuntu and Centos. So, we will start by setting the required inventory variables.

Listing 11-6. Setting Variables for the Apache Configuration files

```
$ echo "apache_cfg: /etc/httpd/conf/httpd.conf" >> $HOME/group_
vars/centos
$ echo "apache_cfg: /etc/apache2/sites-enabled/000-default.
conf" >> \
  $HOME/group_vars/ubuntu
$ ansible-inventory --yaml --host 172.16.120.188
admin_group: sudo
ansible_python_interpreter: /usr/bin/python3
apache_cfg: /etc/apache2/sites-enabled/000-default.conf
apache_pkg: apache2
firewall_pkg: ufw
$ ansible-inventory --yaml --host 172.16.120.161
admin_group: wheel
ansible_connection: local
apache_cfg: /etc/httpd/conf/httpd.conf
apache_pkg: httpd
firewall_pkg: firewalld
```

With the groundwork completed and the variables waiting patiently, we can configure the Apache server and ensure that we add the handler to restart the service on a configuration change.

Listing 11-7. Configuring Apache ServerName

```
$ vim full_apache.yml
- name: Configure Apache
    lineinfile:
      path: "{{ apache_cfg }}"
      line: "ServerName {{ ansible_hostname }}"
      insertafter: "#ServerName"
    notify:
```

```
          - restart_apache
  handlers:
      - name: restart_apache
        service:
          name: "{{ apache_pkg }}"
          state: restarted
```

Configure Filesystem Security

The filesystem security for the Apache HTTP server delivered from either
the CentOS or Ubuntu package is not the best. The web server itself will
gain access through rights granted to *others*. We would be well advised to
remove access to others and allow access through to the Apache user or
group account. This to me seems to be the basics of any security system.
Grant the permissions to smaller groups and not a global group like *others*.
We can use the *file* module in Ansible to set standard permissions or use
the *acl* module to grant permissions though POSIX ACLs. We will use
ACLs, as they offer greater flexibility.

Using POSIX ACLs we can achieve the following filesystem security
advantages:

- **Default ACL**: Adding a default ACL to a directory will
  allow all new files created in the directory to apply
  the default ACL. New files then can have the correct
  permissions without regard to who created the file or
  the current UMASK value.

- **Multiple users and groups**: The standard file mode
  allows for a single user and a single group to be
  assigned permissions. This is why others are used as
  an entity quite often, as more than one user or group
  would need access. Using an ACL, we can assign
  limited or no rights to others and list the required users
  or groups independently.

As the web service will use different user accounts across the differing distributions, we will need to set inventory variables again. On CentOS the user account is *apache* and on Ubuntu the account is *www-data*.

Listing 11-8. Creating Inventory Variable for the Apache User Account

```
$ echo "apache_user: apache" >> $HOME/group_vars/centos
$ echo "apache_user: www-data" >> $HOME/group_vars/ubuntu
$ ansible-inventory --yaml --host 172.16.120.161
admin_group: wheel
ansible_connection: local
apache_cfg: /etc/httpd/conf/httpd.conf
apache_pkg: httpd
apache_user: apache
firewall_pkg: firewalld
$ ansible-inventory --yaml --host 172.16.120.188
admin_group: sudo
ansible_python_interpreter: /usr/bin/python3
apache_cfg: /etc/apache2/sites-enabled/000-default.conf
apache_pkg: apache2
apache_user: www-data
firewall_pkg: ufw
```

Using the *acl* module, we can learn something new. We will use this Ansible module to secure the filesystem used by Apache. We set both the default ACL on the Apache DocumentRoot and including specific permissions for the correct Apache account. The account does not need the write permission and it is not assigned. We remove permissions from the global group others from both the ACL of the directory and the default ACL, so new files will not have access to others when created below the DocumentRoot.

Listing 11-9. Creating an ACL and Default ACL to Secure Apache

```
$ vim full_apache.yml
  - name: Secure default ACL for apache user on document root
    acl:
      path: /var/www/html
      entity: "{{ apache_user }}"
      etype: user
      state: present
      permissions: rx
      default: true
  - name: Secure default ACL for others on document root
    acl:
      path: /var/www/html
      entry: default:others::---
      state: present
  - name: Set read and execute permissions on document root
    for apache user
    acl:
      path: /var/www/html
      entity: "{{ apache_user }}"
      etype: user
      state: present
      permissions: rx
  - name: Set permissions to others to nothing on document
    root
    acl:
      path: /var/www/html
      entry: others::---
      state: present
```

Full Apache Playbook

There has been a lot that we have written for the Playbook. I am sure that your keyboards are crying out for rest, but not quite yet. As promised, we kept the content short by showing just the added elements at each point. We now list the completed Playbook for you.

Listing 11-10. Fill Apache Playbook Listing

```
---
- name: Manage Apache Deployment
  hosts: all
  become: true
  gather_facts: true
  tasks:
    - name:  Install Apache Package
      package:
        name: "{{ apache_pkg }}"
        state: present
    - name: Copy web content
      copy:
        src: web/
        directory_mode: true
        dest: /var/www/html
    - name: Start and Enable Apache Service
      service:
        name: "{{ apache_pkg }}"
        state: started
        enabled: true
    - name: Custom web content
      template:
        src: server.j2
```

```
      dest: /var/www/html/server.html
- name: Firewall Package
  package:
    name: "{{ firewall_pkg }}"
    state: present
- name: Firewall Service
  service:
    name: "{{ firewall_pkg }}"
    enabled: true
    state: started
- name: UFW Ubuntu
  ufw:
      state: enabled
      policy: deny
      rule: allow
      port: "{{ item }}"
      proto: tcp
  loop:
    - "80"
    - "22"
  when: ansible_distribution == "Ubuntu"
- name: Firewalld CentOS
  firewalld:
    service: "{{ item }}"
    permanent: true
    immediate: true
    state: enabled
  loop:
    - "http"
    - "ssh"
  when: ansible_distribution == "CentOS"
```

```
- name: Configure Apache
  lineinfile:
    path: "{{ apache_cfg }}"
    line: "ServerName {{ ansible_hostname }}"
    insertafter: "#ServerName"
  notify:
    - restart_apache
- name: Secure default ACL for apache user on document root
  acl:
    path: /var/www/html
    entity: "{{ apache_user }}"
    etype: user
    state: present
    permissions: rx
    default: true
- name: Secure default ACL for others on document root
  acl:
    path: /var/www/html
    entry: default:others::---
    state: present
- name: Set read and execute permissions on document root
  for apache user
  acl:
    path: /var/www/html
    entity: "{{ apache_user }}"
    etype: user
    state: present
    permissions: rx
- name: Set permissions to others to nothing on document
  root
  acl:
```

```
      path: /var/www/html
      entry: others::---
      state: present
 handlers:
   - name: restart_apache
     service:
       name: "{{ apache_pkg }}"
       state: restarted
...
```

Summary

Deploying your services to a mixed deployment environment is always
a little more complex than you think. It is for this reason we use Ansible,
making sure that everything is always completed and nothing is forgotten.
The more time spent in planning all of the elements that make up the
deployment, the better your deployments will be.

During this chapter we have made a full deployment of Apache by
making sure the software is installed and the service started. With host-
based firewalls being more common to mitigate cyber threats, we also
need to make sure that the correct ports for the service are open. For us,
this meant learning the *ufw* module for Ubuntu and the *firewalld* module
in CentOS. On all systems, we wanted the HTTP port open (we are not
using HTTPS in the book).

By reviewing the use of the *lineinfile* module, we could change the
Apache configuration to have the correct *ServerName* directive configured
to the hostname of each web server. It was good to review this so we could
also see that we can use variables in setting the required line. If you recall,
this is one of my number 1 modules.

We added content to the web servers by copying the content of a directory on the Ansible controller to each web server, the *copy* module and the **directory_mode: true** argument allowing the complete contents to be copied. The custom web page we created using a Jinja 2 template allows specific host information to be displayed. This was delivered with the *template* module.

Correcting some of the weaknesses of the filesystem permission in an Apache deployment, we used the *acl* module in Ansible to configure specific permissions for the correct Apache account. This removed the defaults where others were granted permission to the web page location known as the DocumentRoot in Apache.

CHAPTER 12

Simplifying Playbooks Using Roles

Having everything related to the Apache management in the single Playbook is convenient to a degree, as we have just one file to work with. It is this single file that also provides us with a large and complex amount of data in the one place. By creating smaller code elements, we not only simplify the code, but we also allow for possible code reuse. We will spend our time in this chapter investigating a new command to us, **ansible-galaxy**, which we use to manage roles. In doing so we may well be able to rewrite some code, such as the firewall tasks, so they become more flexible and allow for code reuse in other Playbooks.

Understanding Roles

Roles contain elements of a Playbook such as tasks, variables, and files that are collated within a directory. Roles can be created locally to your own specification or they can be downloaded from the Ansible Galaxy website (we visit the website in the next chapter). These roles contain the necessary components of a Playbook but as individual elements. So instead of one really long Playbook, a role is made from a collection of subdirectories and files. These represent the tasks, handlers, files, templates, variables,

© Andrew Mallett 2021
A. Mallett, *Red Hat Certified Engineer (RHCE) Study Guide*,
https://doi.org/10.1007/978-1-4842-6861-2_12

and so on that would otherwise be used in a monolithic Playbook. Roles are managed via the **ansible-galaxy** command. Subcommands from the command are listed as follows:

- *init*: Creates the required structure for a role

- *list*: Lists roles within the path structure

- *search*: Searches for roles on the Galaxy repository

- *install*: Downloads and installs a role from the URL

- *remove*: Removes a role from the system

Roles can be created on a per-user basis in the directory in *$HOME/.ansible/roles* or can be shared between users on the controller in the */etc/ansible/roles* or */usr/share/ansible/roles* directories. We will not have any roles on the system to start with; roles are not installed by default with Ansible. The *$HOME/.ansible/roles* directory does not exist by default either, so we do start with a pretty bleak outlook. Don't worry though, this will quickly change. Let's try listing the roles and see what happens:

Listing 12-1. Listing Ansible Roles

```
$ ansible-galaxy list
# /usr/share/ansible/roles
# /etc/ansible/roles
[WARNING]: - the configured path /home/tux/.ansible/roles does
not exist.
```

OK, so nothing. I did not lie to you and we get the warning that the directory does not exist. We do not need to do anything at the moment, as we can create the required directory along with our roles. Speaking of which, let's look at our first role and see what **ansible-galaxy** is all about.

Creating Firewall Role

As we have seen with the *full_ansible.yml* Playbook, the lines required for the firewall elements are quite extensive. Removing the code from the Playbook relating to the firewall not only will make the Playbook more readable and succinct but will additionally allow for code reuse. Rather than hard-coding the port or service that we want to open up in the firewall, we will use a variable. This variable can then be populated within the calling play and not be stored with the role. We really do get the double benefit with this role straightaway: clarity of code and the ability to reuse that saved code in other plays and Playbooks. We will work from the Apache project directory that we have been working within for a little while and begin by creating a new role for the firewall.

Listing 12-2. Creating the Firewall Role

```
$ cd $HOME/ansible/apache
$ ansible-galaxy role init $HOME/.ansible/roles/firewall
- Role /home/tux/.ansible/roles/firewall was created
  successfully
$ $ tree $HOME/.ansible/roles/firewall
/home/tux/.ansible/roles/firewall
├── defaults
│   └── main.yml
├── files
├── handlers
│   └── main.yml
├── meta
│   └── main.yml
├── README.md
├── tasks
│   └── main.yml
```

```
├── templates
├── tests
│   ├── inventory
│   └── test.yml
└── vars
    └── main.yml
        dest: /var/www/html/server.html
$ ansible-galaxy list
# /home/tux/.ansible/roles
- firewall, (unknown version)
# /usr/share/ansible/roles
# /etc/ansible/roles
```

Populating the Firewall Role

The firewall role is now created and does show when listing the roles
that we have installed on the system. The role can be shared between
Playbooks and is not limited to any particular YAML file. Using the **tree**
command, we can see the subdirectory structure and the associated files.
We can add the tasks that should be used with the role to the *main.yml*
file in the roles's *tasks* subdirectory. We **only** add the tasks and **not** the
plays to this file. Additionally, we will use a new variable in the task to
define the service we require opening in the firewall. We will not define the
variable in the role, as we want the role to work with any service and not
just Apache. The variable will be set from the calling play in the Playbook.
First, we will create the role content by editing *the $HOME/.ansible/roles/
firewall/tasks/main.yml* file. The content that we add can be first removed
from the *full_apache.yml* before being copied to the *main.yml*. Take care to
remove unnecessary indents from the copied data; each task will now be a
list item at the root level of the file.

Note   It is probably wise to make a backup copy of the *full_apache.yml* before deleting the redundant lines. It is easy to delete too many lines, and being able to revert to a saved version is always a comforting option.

Listing 12-3. Populating the Firewall Role tasks/main.yml File

```
$ vim $HOME/.ansible/roles/firewall/tasks/main.yml
---
- name: Firewall Package
  package:
    name: "{{ firewall_pkg }}"
    state: present
- name: Firewall Service
  service:
    name: "{{ firewall_pkg }}"
    enabled: true
    state: started
- name: UFW Ubuntu
  ufw:
      state: enabled
      policy: deny
      rule: allow
      port: "{{ item }}"
  loop:
    - "{{ service_name }}"
    - "ssh"
  when: ansible_distribution == "Ubuntu"
- name: Firewalld CentOS
  firewalld:
```

```
    service: "{{ item }}"
    permanent: true
    immediate: true
    state: enabled
  loop:
    - "{{ service_name }}"
    - "ssh"
  when: ansible_distribution == "CentOS"
...
```

Note   The *ufw* module port argument can take a service name or port number. We standardize on using the service name for ease in these examples. We always want SSH enabled, which we have hard-coded to the list of services.

These 31 lines have been removed from the original Playbook and can now be used independently. This single role can work by opening the correct port for MySQL, Redis, SMTP, or any required port.

Updating the Apache Playbook

The original Playbook will still operate without the deleted lines that relate to the firewall; however, we still want to ensure that the firewall is configured correctly on each managed device. Within our play, we can add a new list of roles. We must also set the *service_name* variable that is used by the role. Having made sure that we have removed the tasks relating to the firewall configuration from the *full_apache.yml* Playbook, we can reedit it, setting the variable and referencing the role. To reduce the output display, we list only the play details and the list of roles, not the tasks or handlers.

Listing 12-4. Editing the full_apache.yml Playbook to Reference the Role

```
$ vim   $HOME/ansible/apache/full_apache.yml
---
- name: Manage Apache Deployment
  hosts: all
  become: true
  gather_facts: true
  vars:
    - service_name: http
  roles:
    - firewall
```

We have two new lists: the list of variables and the lists of roles. The firewall related tasks have been removed, but this is not displayed. Configuring the *service_name* variable within this play, we will enable the HTTP port within the firewall role. We are not limited to just the one port that we open; we could easily create another play within the same Playbook to set another port such as MySQL. The variable for each play is independent of the other. Implementing this process will allow us to deploy a full LAMP, Linux, Apache, MySQL, and PHP server and reuse shared code, with the firewall role opening both HTTP and MySQL ports.

Configure Role for Web Content

It is eminently possible that different web server configurations will need different web content. Is this a marketing web server or is it an IT web server? By having different roles for content, we can include the correct content role with the Apache Playbook. In doing so, we can also learn to use different elements of the role, and we introduce the *files* and *templates* directory. To deliver the correct files to managed devices, those files should be added to the *files* subdirectory of the role. In delivering the template, we add the server.j2 file to the role's *templates* subdirectory. In this way, the files and YAML code are better organized and more easily identified and located. We start by creating a new role called *standard_web*.

Listing 12-5. Adding Files and Templates to New Web Content Role

```
$ ansible-galaxy role init /home/tux/.ansible/roles/standard_web
- Role /home/tux/.ansible/roles/standard_web was created
  successfully
$ mv $HOME/ansible/apache/web $HOME/.ansible/roles/standard_
  web/files/
$ mv $HOME/ansible/apache/server.j2 \ $HOME/.ansible/roles/
  standard_web/templates/
$ tree /home/tux/.ansible/roles/standard_web/
/home/tux/.ansible/roles/standard_web/
├── defaults
│   └── main.yml
├── files
│   └── web
│       ├── contact.html
│       └── index.html
├── handlers
│   └── main.yml
├── meta
│   └── main.yml
├── README.md
├── tasks
│   └── main.yml
├── templates
│   └── server.j2
```

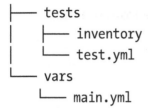

```
├── tests
│   ├── inventory
│   └── test.yml
└── vars
    └── main.yml
```

Browsing the output from the **tree** command, we can see how the new *standard_web* role should appear with the newly added content. We again need to work with the *main.yml* file with the *tasks* subdirectory. We will remove the tasks related to content from the *full_apache.yml* Playbook, adding them to the *standard_web* role.

Listing 12-6. Adding Tasks to the standard_web Role tasks/main.yml

```
$ vim $HOME/.ansible/standard_web/tasks/main.yml
---
- name: Copy web content
  copy:
    src: web/
    directory_mode: true
    dest: /var/www/html
- name: Custom web content
  template:
    src: server.j2
    dest: /var/www/html/server.html
```

We take care in removing these lines from the *full_apache.yml* Playbook and adding them to the role. Each task is added as a list item at the root level of the file's indentation. Take great care to ensure that you maintain the correct indentation level for the module and module arguments. The module should be at the same level as the task name and the arguments indented below the module. With this very carefully prepared, we can now return to the *full_apache* Playbook and include the new role.

Listing 12-7. Referencing the Web Content Role from the full_
apache.yml Playbook

```
$ vim  $HOME/ansible/apache/full_apache.yml
---
- name: Manage Apache Deployment
  hosts: all
  become: true
  gather_facts: true
  vars:
    - service_name: http
  roles:
    - firewall
    - standard_web
```

We can now start seeing the benefits that we can harvest from using
roles. We have reduced the number of lines within the Playbook, making
it easier to read and manage. These lines still exist but have now been
farmed out to roles, which can be used in many different Playbooks if
required.

Creating the Apache Role

The tasks and handlers that remain in the *full_apache.yml* probably can
exist together within the final role. This role will install the web package
and start the service. That service will need the ServerName directive
setting, and we should secure the DocumentRoot. Although they could
be separate, these events should all happen if the web server is installed,
which is why we set these tasks as a single role. As before, these deleted
tasks will be added to the *main.yml* below the *tasks* subdirectory of the
new role. We will also be able to add the handler to the new role's *handlers*
subdirectory.

Listing 12-8. Creating and Populating the Apache Role

```
$ ansible-galaxy role init $HOME/.ansible/roles/apache
- Role /home/tux/.ansible/roles/apache was created successfully
$ vim $HOME/.ansible/roles/apache/tasks/main.yml
---
- name:  Install Apache Package
  package:
    name: "{{ apache_pkg }}"
    state: present
- name: Start and Enable Apache Service
  service:
    name: "{{ apache_pkg }}"
    state: started
    enabled: true
- name: Configure Apache
  lineinfile:
    path: "{{ apache_cfg }}"
    line: "ServerName {{ ansible_hostname }}"
    insertafter: "#ServerName"
  notify:
    - restart_apache
- name: Secure default ACL for apache user on document root
  acl:
    path: /var/www/html
    entity: "{{ apache_user }}"
    etype: user
    state: present
    permissions: rx
    default: true
- name: Secure default ACL for others on document root
  acl:
```

```
    path: /var/www/html
    entry: default:others::---
    state: present
- name: Set read and execute permissions on document root for
  apache user
  acl:
    path: /var/www/html
    entity: "{{ apache_user }}"
    etype: user
    state: present
    permissions: rx
- name: Set permissions to others to nothing on document root
  acl:
    path: /var/www/html
    entry: others::---
    state: present
```

$ **vim $HOME/.ansible/roles/apache/handlers/main.yml**

```
---

- name: restart_apache
  service:
    name: "{{ apache_pkg }}"
    state: restarted
```

$ **vim $HOME/ansible/apache/full_apache.yml**

```
---

- name: Manage Apache Deployment
  hosts: all
  become: true
  gather_facts: true
  vars:
    - service_name: http
  roles:
```

```
- apache
- firewall
- standard_web
```

We now list the **complete** *full_apache* Playbook, which is now just 11 lines long. Yes, just 11 lines where it had previously been 92 lines! The simplicity of the Playbook is now so beautiful to behold, with each element being moved to a more concise and specific file.

Execution Order

If you pay careful attention to the roles that we have now added, we made sure that the *apache* role is listed first. If we have tasks and roles listed in the play, they will play in the order in which they are listed or written in the play. If the tasks are listed first, they will execute first; if the roles are listed first, the roles will execute first. Likewise, each role or task is executed in the order of the list definition. Within our roles, we need to have the Apache web server installed before we add web content to it. Although it may not appear to matter with our current systems, as everything was already in place, on new systems added to the inventory we do need to take care and consider the execution order.

Summary

Roles are one of the most useful elements that you will use with Ansible. By implementing roles, we are making that big step forward to code reuse. We discard and put behind us the monolithic Playbooks we have created in the past and we see a new dawn of productivity.

We became a little familiar with the command **ansible-galaxy** to create and list roles. Using the *init* subcommand, we can create the filesystem structure needed by the role. This is optional, as we could create the directories and files ourselves but, frankly, I love the convenience of not having to create them myself. Adding roles to the *$HOME/.ansible/roles* directory allows the roles we create to be available to use from any of our Playbooks, in much the same way as we use the *$HOME/.ansible.cfg* file to share across Playbook projects.

We started by creating a firewall role and making it more useful by allowing a variable to control the port we need to open. We need to list the role and the variable that we set within the play for ease of use. Next we created the web content role, which we use to add the standard web pages and custom content from the template. This role will make use of both files and templates, and the role organizes these files within their own subdirectories. Organization of your code and files is paramount with roles. Finally, we learned how we can use both tasks and handlers within a role when we created a role to deploy the Apache web server—tasks being organized with their own directory, and the same with handlers.

The original line count of the Playbook was reduced from 92 lines to just 11. Sure, the code has not simply disappeared; it has been added to three new roles, but we can share these roles between Playbooks. In this chapter we have learned the basics of roles by creating our own. In the next chapter we will learn to search and download prewritten roles to save us the effort. Remember that big retort, *why reinvent the wheel*?

CHAPTER 13

Downloading Roles

We are not limited to the roles that we create ourselves, far from it. We can download community created roles and freely use them on our own system. You will find these roles are hosted on the `https://galaxy.ansible.com` website, which you can browse from the command line or graphically through a web browser. In this chapter we will continue developing our Apache Playbook by adding PHP and MySQL to make a LAMP server, Linux Apache, MySQL(MariaDB), and PHP.

Roles and Collections

For the RHCE exam EX294, you should only need to know about roles and not collections. The current exam objectives state: "*This exam is based on Red Hat Enterprise Linux 8 and Red Hat Ansible Engine 2.8.*" We are using Ansible version 2.9.x and we now have both roles and collections. Collections are simply, collections of roles, and the technology does not really change. Collections can make organizing related roles a little easier and provides a simple single download. We will be working with roles within this chapter to add PHP and MySQL. This will be a superficial look at roles but concentrating on searching and downloading the required roles. We will also be able to look at a couple of new standalone tasks contained in a code block, so there's lots to look forward to.

© Andrew Mallett 2021
A. Mallett, *Red Hat Certified Engineer (RHCE) Study Guide*,
https://doi.org/10.1007/978-1-4842-6861-2_13

Searching Roles From the CLI

When working from the CLI or the command line environment of the Ansible controller, we can use **ansible-galaxy** to search for roles located within the Galaxy repository. If we just search for a module name, we may find that we have too many results to choose from. Remember that these are community created. Knowing a reliable author can help, and we can add the author name to the search. Having located a possible match, we can use the *info* subcommand to list more detail. Like always, and as we have promoted throughout this book, we want you to get hands-on practice in your own lab environment. This will help you to become proficient both at work and in the exam.

Listing 13-1. Searching for Roles from the CLI

```
$ ansible-galaxy search php
Found 1075 roles matching your search. Showing first 1000.
...
$ ansible-galaxy search --author geerlingguy php
Found 24 roles matching your search:
...
$ ansible-galaxy info geerlingguy.php
...
```

When looking at the output provided by the info subcommand, the *download count* can help you understand the popularity of the role. The author listed here is very well respected in the community and I use his modules myself. The command line is OK, but the web front end to Galaxy offers much more detail on the roles. Browsing the https://galaxy.ansible.com website is simple and provides access to the role's readme file, which is more detailed than the simple *info* output we see at the command line. Try visiting the website and locating the same PHP module.

Installing the PHP Role

Installing these oven-ready roles saves us the hassle and time of creating our own roles. We could certainly install PHP ourselves, but the roles save us from researching the package names. We can also make changes to the PHP settings if needed.

- ***php***: The PHP script engine for use at the command line or with a web server

Listing 13-2. Installing PHP Role on the Ansible Controller Node

```
$ ansible-galaxy install geerlingguy.php
- downloading role 'php', owned by geerlingguy
- downloading role from https://github.com/geerlingguy/ansible-
  role-php/archive/4.5.1.tar.gz
- extracting geerlingguy.php to /home/tux/.ansible/roles/
  geerlingguy.php
- geerlingguy.php (4.5.1) was installed successfully- Role
$ ansible-galaxy list
# /home/tux/.ansible/roles
- firewall, (unknown version)
- standard_web, (unknown version)
- apache, (unknown version)
- geerlingguy.php, 4.5.1
# /usr/share/ansible/roles
# /etc/ansible/roles
```

Investigating PHP Role and Learning Better Coding

The default path to install the role to is *$HOME/.ansible/roles/*; if you need to install to a different location, you will need to use the option **--roles-path**. We can list the contents of the role using the **tree** command.

Listing 13-3. Listing the Role

```
$ tree /home/tux/.ansible/roles/geerlingguy.php/
/home/tux/.ansible/roles/geerlingguy.php/
├── defaults
│   └── main.yml
├── handlers
│   └── main.yml
├── LICENSE
├── meta
│   └── main.yml
├── molecule
│   └── default
│       ├── converge.yml
│       ├── molecule.yml
│       ├── playbook-source.yml
│       └── requirements.yml
├── README.md
├── tasks
│   ├── configure-apcu.yml
│   ├── configure-fpm.yml
│   ├── configure-opcache.yml
│   ├── configure.yml
│   ├── install-from-source.yml
│   ├── main.yml
│   ├── setup-Debian.yml
│   └── setup-RedHat.yml
├── templates
│   ├── apc.ini.j2
│   ├── fpm-init.j2
│   ├── opcache.ini.j2
│   ├── php-fpm.conf.j2
│
```

```
|       ├── php.ini.j2
|       └── www.conf.j2
└── vars
        ├── Debian-10.yml
        ├── Debian-9.yml
        ├── Debian.yml
        ├── RedHat.yml
        ├── Ubuntu-16.yml
        ├── Ubuntu-18.yml
        └── Ubuntu-20.yml
```

Taking our research and learning a little further, we can begin the journey into writing better code. The *tasks* directory contains many YAML files, and not just the *main.yml* file. To learn how this can work, let's list the contents *main.yml*. It is certainly worth taking our time to look at the complete file; we just list part of it for clarity of output in the book.

Listing 13-4. The Tasks default.yml Includes Other YAML Files

```
$ grep -A10 Setup $HOME/.ansible/roles/geerlingguy.php/tasks/
main.yml
# Setup/install tasks.
- include_tasks: setup-RedHat.yml
  when:
    - not php_install_from_source
    - ansible_os_family == 'RedHat'

- include_tasks: setup-Debian.yml
  when:
    - not php_install_from_source
    - ansible_os_family == 'Debian'
```

We can see that the author, Jeff Geerling, includes additional tasks from the specialist distribution files working with Red Hat, Ubuntu, and Debian-based systems. CentOS is part of the Red Hat OS Family. We can dig further into the Red Hat file and see what will be executed. It is always worth researching this; after all it is going to be our systems in which the code runs. We want to be certain that the correct actions will take place, and we can learn by viewing the code from others. This is a fundamental premise of open source code.

Listing 13-5. Listing the Red Hat Tasks

```
$ cat $HOME/.ansible/roles/geerlingguy.php/tasks/setup-RedHat.yml
---
- name: Ensure PHP packages are installed.
  package:
    name: "{{ php_packages + php_packages_extra }}"
    state: "{{ php_packages_state }}"
    enablerepo: "{{ php_enablerepo | default(omit, true) }}"
  notify: restart webserver
```

As the web server needs to be restarted after PHP has been added, we can see that we notify a handler to complete this. The handler is organized separately from the tasks in their own directory. We saw this previously with our own Apache role.

Listing 13-6. Listing Handlers in the PHP Role

```
$ cat $HOME/.ansible/roles/geerlingguy.php/handlers/main.yml
---
- name: restart webserver
  service:
    name: "{{ php_webserver_daemon }}"
    state: restarted
```

```
  notify: restart php-fpm
  when: php_enable_webserver

- name: restart php-fpm
  service:
    name: "{{ php_fpm_daemon }}"
    state: "{{ php_fpm_handler_state }}"
  when:
    - php_enable_php_fpm
    - php_fpm_state == 'started'
```

There are many variables in use throughout this role; for example, we can see the web server that will be restarted is the variable *php_webserver_ daemon*. We can search this further in the *vars* subdirectory of the role.

Listing 13-7. Listing Role Variables

```
$ grep php_webserver_daemon \
  $HOME/.ansible/roles/geerlingguy.php/vars/RedHat.yml
__php_webserver_daemon: "httpd"
```

We also can control these variables from our Playbook or inventory. We will use a variable to ensure that we do link PHP to the web server, for example. We will see this in the very next section.

Installing PHP

Now we are, at least, a little familiar with the role and we can add it to the *full_apache.yml* Playbook. We will set the PHP variables to link to the web server and create a simple PHP page so we can test the operation of PHP.

Listing 13-8. Installing PHP from the Role

```
$ vim $HOME/ansible/apache/full_apache.yml
---
- name: Manage Apache Deployment
  hosts: all
  become: true
  gather_facts: true
  vars:
    - service_name: http
    - php_enable_webserver: true
  roles:
    - apache
    - firewall
    - standard_web
    - geerlingguy.php
  tasks:
    - name: add php page
      copy:
        dest: /var/www/html/test.php
        content: "<?php phpinfo(); ?>"
```

After running your Playbook, you will have PHP installed and the web server will have restarted. It was the variable implemented in the Playbook that enables the handler to run. To test this, you should use a browser on your host system and point it to the IP address of your host; for me this would be: http://172.16.120.161/test.php. You should see a colored table illustrating the configuration of your web server and PHP.

Note   The *test.php* file should display correctly on CentOS. There is a little more work needed on Ubuntu, which we will add later in the chapter when we investigate code blocks in Ansible.

Adding Extra PHP Modules

In a lab environment we will eventually need to connect from the PHP code running on Apache through to our database server. Jeff Geerling, (geerlingguy), does have a role for this but it is not updated for CentOS 8. We could modify the *geerlingguy.php-msql* role to suit our needs; however, it is easy to install the required package. In doing so, we can demonstrate that we can make use of the handler within the PHP role to restart the web server after installation of the required module. We do not need to create our own handler.

The required PHP packages that we need to install for both CentOS 8 and Ubuntu 18.04 are listed as follows:

- **CentOS 8**: php-mysqlnd

- **Ubuntu 18:04**: php7.2-mysql

We are well aware by now of our inventory variables, and it is easy to add these package names to the correct files group files. This we demonstrate now. But don't forget, you are meant to be following along in your own labs, so don't just read; you need to *read* and *practice*!

Listing 13-9. Adding Correct PHP MySQL Packages to the Systems, Allowing PHP to Talk to the Database Server

```
$ echo "php_mysql: php7.2-mysql" >> $HOME/group_vars/ubuntu
$ echo "php_mysql: php-mysqlnd" >> $HOME/group_vars/centos
$ ansible-inventory --yaml --host 172.16.120.188
admin_group: sudo
ansible_python_interpreter: /usr/bin/python3
apache_cfg: /etc/apache2/sites-enabled/000-default.conf
apache_pkg: apache2
apache_user: www-data
firewall_pkg: ufw
```

```
php_mysql: php7.2-mysql
$ ansible-inventory --yaml --host 172.16.120.161
admin_group: wheel
ansible_connection: local
apache_cfg: /etc/httpd/conf/httpd.conf
apache_pkg: httpd
apache_user: apache
firewall_pkg: firewalld
php_mysql: php-mysqlnd
$ vim full_apache.yml
---
- name: Manage Apache Deployment
  hosts: all
  become: true
  gather_facts: true
  vars:
    - service_name: http
    - php_enable_webserver: true
  roles:
    - apache
    - firewall
    - standard_web
    - geerlingguy.php
  tasks:
    - name: add php page
      copy:
        dest: /var/www/html/test.php
        content: "<?php phpinfo(); ?>"
    - name: Install mysql-php
      package:
        name: "{{ php_mysql }}"
      notify: restart webserver
```

This time we set the variables within the group inventory and not the play itself. The values needed will be different, based on the host's distribution, so it is best suited to the inventory. The task will restart the web server; the handler for that is within the *geerlingguy.php* role and there is no need to redefine the handler.

Code Blocks and Extra Configuration for Ubuntu

Installing Apache on Ubuntu 18.04 does not install the PHP Apache module by default. We need to install and enable the Apache module. Ideally, we would add this to the Apache role specifically for Apache, but there is an argument that would suggest not to install modules in Apache that you don't need. Not every Apache server will need to run PHP. For the moment, we will add tasks to the existing play so we can demonstrate using code blocks within Ansible. A code block is an additional indentation level that can contain one or more tasks. We need to add two additional tasks that we can add to the block, adding the **when** clause to the code block to ensure it only runs on Ubuntu. The restriction is defined at the code block level and will affect all tasks in the block.

Note   The **when** clause can be added to a code block but the **notify** operator is not compatible with a block; we add the **notify** operator to each task.

Listing 13-10. Adding Code Blocks to Finalize Ubuntu Apache PHP Installation

```
$ vim full_apache.yml
---
- name: Manage Apache Deployment
  hosts: all
```

```
become: true
gather_facts: true
vars:
  - service_name: http
  - php_enable_webserver: true
roles:
  - apache
  - firewall
  - standard_web
  - geerlingguy.php
tasks:
  - name: add php page
    copy:
      dest: /var/www/html/test.php
      content: "<?php phpinfo(); ?>"
  - name: Install mysql-php
    package:
      name: "{{ php_mysql }}"
    notify: restart webserver
  - name: Add Apache PHP and Enable on Ubuntu
    block:
      - name: Install Apache PHP Module
        apt:
          name: libapache2-mod-php
          state: present
        notify: restart webserver
      - name: Enable PHP Module
        apache2_module:
          state: present
          name: php7.2
        notify: restart web server
    when: ansible_distribution == "Ubuntu"
```

The Apache module is both installed and enabled with the *apt* module. We know we are using this only on Ubuntu, so *apt* is used rather than *package*. As a double-check, we independently enable the module using the *apache2_module*. This covers situations where the Apache module is manually disabled; in this way we ensure that the module is both installed and enabled, no matter what occurs.

We now have Apache and PHP installed and running on each system. We will soon install the database server, but for the moment just make sure you can display the *info.php* page on each system. Remember, this should show an extensive page with graphics and colored table columns.

Install the Database Role

You might notice that I have not been explicit with the Database server that we are installing. I am not trying to be secretive but will use Jeff Geerling's mysql module. On CentOS 8 it will install MariaDB and on Ubuntu 18.04 it will install MySQL. Both will work for us, but we again highlight the differences in distributions and the advantages of learning Ansible on more than one Linux flavor.

Create Variable File

Instead of adding the variables directly to the Playbook as we have done so far, we will use a *vars_file:* argument just as we did with **ansible-vault**. We do not need an encrypted file to use the *vars_file:* argument, and this is demonstrated to you. We do store the MySQL root password in the variable file, so do consider encrypting the file. The more practice you can gather, the better prepared you will be for the exam. You have done an awesome job so far and you do not want to forget anything that you have previously looked at.

Listing 13-11. Creating Variables for MySQL

```
$ vim $HOME/ansible/apache ; mkdir vars
$ vim vars/main.yml
---
mysql_root_password: Password1
mysql_root_password_update: true
mysql_enabled_on_startup: true
mysql_users:
  - name: bob
    host: "%"
    password: Password1
    priv: "*.*:ALL"
```

The variables are used with a new role that we will download shortly. Most of the variables are quite self-explanatory, but we do create a new user on each database server. To aid the creation of that user, we define a dictionary for each element needed. We set the database user's name, we allow access from any host for that user, set their password, and allow access to all databases. Having an additional account is useful for our testing, as the MySQL root account should not be able to log on from anywhere other than the localhost for security reasons.

Installing the MySQL Role and Implementing a Database Server

We can now download the *mysql* role and reference both the role and variable file from the Playbook. As always, we should test the Playbook at each stage. So please run the Playbook after editing it; you will be immensely pleased when you see it run. Believe me; you have this covered!

Listing 13-12. Downloading and Using the mysql Role

```
$ ansible-galaxy install geerlingguy.mysql
$ vim  $HOME/ansible/apache/full_apache.yml
---
- name: Manage Apache Deployment
  hosts: all
  become: true
  gather_facts: true
  vars:
    - service_name: http
    - php_enable_webserver: true
  vars_files:
    - vars/main.yml
  roles:
    - apache
    - firewall
    - standard_web
    - geerlingguy.php
    - geerlingguy.mysql
  tasks:
    - name: add php page
      copy:
        dest: /var/www/html/test.php
        content: "<?php phpinfo(); ?>"
    - name: Install mysql-php
      package:
        name: "{{ php_mysql }}"
      notify: restart webserver
    - name: Add Apache PHP and Enable on Ubuntu
      block:
        - name: Install Apache PHP Module
```

```
      apt:
        name: libapache2-mod-php
        state: present
      notify: restart webserver
    - name: Enable PHP Module
      apache2_module:
        state: present
        name: php7.2
      notify: restart web server
  when: ansible_distribution == "Ubuntu"
```

Testing the Playbook now should show the installation of the Database server and the creation of the new database user.

Opening MySQL Firewall Port

We will be able to connect locally as *root* and *bob*, but we will need to open the database port on each system's firewall to connect as bob remotely. We can use the existing *firewall* role that we created earlier. We will create an additional play to allow us to execute the role again with a new service definition. The second play can be added to the existing Playbook. For ease we add it as the *first play*, but it does not matter if it is the first or second play. For me, using it as the first play means that I only need to list the top of the Playbook for you to see what was added.

Listing 13-13. Adding a New Play to the Existing Playbook

```
$ vim full_apache.yml
---
# New Play 1
- name: Enable MySQL Port
  hosts: all
  gather_facts: true
```

```
  become: true
  vars:
    - service_name: mysql
  roles:
    - firewall
# Existing Play is now Play 2
- name: Manage Apache Deployment
```

We have now completed a full LAMP installation and we will be able to test the database connectivity from the command line. We should be able to connect as the MySQL bob user to each host from our controller. Adjust the following to match your own lab IP addresses. We connect as the new user and list the standard databases that are hosted on each system.

Listing 13-14. Testing Database Connectivity

```
$ mysql  -h 172.16.120.188 -u bob -pPassword1 -e "SHOW DATABASES;"
+--------------------+
| Database           |
+--------------------+
| information_schema |
| mysql              |
| performance_schema |
| sys                |
+--------------------+
$ mysql  -h 172.16.120.185 -u bob -pPassword1 -e "SHOW DATABASES;"
+--------------------+
| Database           |
+--------------------+
| information_schema |
| mysql              |
| performance_schema |
+--------------------+
```

```
$ mysql  -h 172.16.120.161 -u bob -pPassword1 -e "SHOW DATABASES;"
+--------------------+
| Database           |
+--------------------+
| information_schema |
| mysql              |
| performance_schema |
+--------------------+
```

I am hoping this was successful for you. If not, carefully read any errors and check the Playbook and variable files. It is really worthwhile to stick with this to get this working.

Summary

Wow, look what you have done! The one Playbook will now reliably install the full LAMP stack on CentOS 8 and Ubuntu 18.04. Nothing will be forgotten, and this is repeatably correct. We have met the nirvana of configuration management; just stop and absorb this a little before you continue.

We had previously seen that we can create our own roles, and that was very good for us as we have been honing our Ansible skills. So, it did make sense that we build on those skills in developing the initial roles that we created. Now that we have these skills, we can learn that there are many community-created roles to save our effort. However, if we don't understand Ansible, the roles are not so useful, so your learning has not been wasted in any way, shape, or form.

We looked at new modules in this chapter too. We used the *apt* module specifically for Ubuntu and the *apache_module* Ansible module that is used to enable and disable Apache modules in Ubuntu. This led us to learning about code blocks, allowing us to isolate tasks to a specific **when** clause.

The final solution that we have created is something you should keep and archive. This is a valuable resource and should not be wasted; you will want to keep this I am sure for future use.

CHAPTER 14

Configuring Storage with Ansible

There are many items in Linux, as well as many other systems, that we can manage using Ansible. We have concentrated on managing the web server in the demonstrations so far, and I am truly hopeful this has helped your learning of Ansible configuration management. We will now tack differently and take a look at managing the storage subsystem in Linux. We will learn to partition disks, and create logical volumes before creating filesystems and mounting those filesystems. New from CentOS 7.5 is VDO, the Virtual Data Optimizer. Using VDO we can learn how to create volumes that are enabled for compression and data deduplication, and of course this will be managed with Ansible.

Note Demonstrations in the chapter will take place using the controller node only, due to the fact that we need to add additional block storage to the node. You are welcome to add the storage to each node or deploy your systems with additional unused storage.

© Andrew Mallett 2021
A. Mallett, *Red Hat Certified Engineer (RHCE) Study Guide*,
https://doi.org/10.1007/978-1-4842-6861-2_14

Block Devices

We certainly could add additional virtual disks to our controller to make more block devices available to us. We can, alternatively, create loopback devices in Linux implementing virtual block devices. This is easier than adding external disks, as we perform this all from the Linux command line where we have available free disk space. My controller defaulted to a 20GB drive, leaving me 15GB free space, which is more than enough. We will add additional block devices to support the exercises, using a 5GB disk for VDO, as a minimum size of 4GB is required.

Creating Loopback Devices

A loopback device is an internal virtual block device in Linux. We can use this to mount ISO files to loopback devices as an example. For the labs, we will create raw files and then connect them as loopback devices. To list current block devices in Linux, we can use the command **lsblk**.

Listing 14-1. Listing Block Devices in Linux from the CLI

```
$ lsblk
NAME           MAJ:MIN RM   SIZE RO TYPE MOUNTPOINT
sda              8:0    0    20G  0 disk
├─sda1           8:1    0     1G  0 part /boot
└─sda2           8:2    0    19G  0 part
  ├─cl-root 253:0    0    17G  0 lvm  /
  └─cl-swap 253:1    0     2G  0 lvm  [SWAP]
sr0             11:0    1   6.7G  0 rom
```

Reviewing the **TYPE** column, we see *disks, partitions, logical volumes,* and a CD-ROM. Currently we do not have *loop* devices. If we had listed *loop* devices, we could list them independently with the **losetup** command. Without *loop* devices, the output of **losetup** will be empty.

Listing 14-2. Listing Loop Devices in Linux Using losetup

```
$ losetup
```

The first step in creating a loop device is to create the back-end file to use as storage. This is created with either the command **dd** or **fallocate**. We use **fallocate** because it is quicker.

Listing 14-3. Creating a 1GB Raw Disk File Using fallocate

```
$ cd $HOME/ansible ; mkdir disk ; cd disk
$ fallocate -l 1G disk0 # The option is -l for length
$ ls -lh disk0
-rw-rw-r--. 1 tux tux 1.0G Dec 10 13:59 disk0
```

Reviewing the demonstrated commands, we first create a new Ansible project directory before creating a 1GB file with **fallocate** within the disk project directory. We can now use this raw file to be linked to a *loop* device. Currently we do not have any loop devices, making the first available device */dev/loop0*.

Listing 14-4. Creating Our First Linux Loop Device

```
$ sudo losetup /dev/loop0 disk0
$ losetup
NAME        SIZELIMIT OFFSET AUTOCLEAR RO BACK-
FILE                       DIO LOG-SEC
/dev/loop0        0      0          0 0 /home/tux/ansible/
disk/disk0  0     512
$ lsblk
NAME        MAJ:MIN RM  SIZE RO TYPE MOUNTPOINT
loop0          7:0   0   1G  0 loop
sda            8:0   0  20G  0 disk
├─sda1         8:1   0   1G  0 part /boot
```

```
└─sda2           8:2    0   19G  0 part
  ├─cl-root 253:0    0   17G  0 lvm  /
  └─cl-swap 253:1    0    2G  0 lvm  [SWAP]
sr0             11:0    1  6.7G  0 rom
```

Listing *loop* devices with **losetup** now shows our new block device, as does the **lsblk** command. We can use */dev/loop0* in the same way as any read/write block device. This is where we start to engage with Ansible as we look at partitioning this device.

Partitioning Disks and Mounting Filesystems

We will use Ansible to add a new partition before adding an XFS filesystem to it and mounting the filesystem to a newly created directory. Mounting the partition will also add an entry to the */etc/fstab* file to persist the filesystems on reboot. As we are quite familiar with Ansible now, we will create a complete new Playbook in the disk project directory with all the required tasks.

Note   The hosts argument in the play should be set to the IP address of your controller node used in the inventory.

Listing 14-5. Partitioning Disk and Mounting filesystem with Ansible

```
$ vim partition.yml
- name: Partition disk/filesystem/mount
  hosts: 172.16.120.161
  gather_facts: no
```

```yaml
    become: true
    tasks:
      - name: Partition loop0 P1
        parted:
          device: /dev/loop0
          part_start: 0%
          part_end: 50%
          number: 1
          state: present
      - name: Create XFS filesystem on P1
        filesystem:
          dev: /dev/loop0p1
          fstype: xfs
      - name: Create mount point
        file:
          path: "{{ item }}"
          state: directory
        loop:
          - /data
          - /data/p1
      - name: Mount P1 to /data/p1
        mount:
          path: /data/p1
          src: /dev/loop0p1
          fstype: xfs
          state: mounted
```

```
$ ansible-playbook partition.yml
$ tail -n1 /etc/fstab
/dev/loop0p1 /data/p1 xfs defaults 0 0
$ mount -t xfs
```

```
/dev/mapper/cl-root on / type xfs
(rw,relatime,seclabel,attr2,inode64,noquota)
/dev/loop0p1 on /data/p1 type xfs (rw,relatime,seclabel,attr2,i
node64,noquota)
```

Now that we are getting proficient in creating these Playbooks, it is probably quicker to run these tasks via the Playbook than using the raw commands at the command line. The Ansible modules used are listed for you now:

- **parted**: Used in much the same way as the parted command at the command line. We can use this module to create and add partitions on a disk.

- **filesystem**: Used to format the block device

- **file**: The file module to ensure the present or absence of a file and attributes. Here we ensure that they are directories.

- **mount**: The mount module is used to mount or unmount filesystems and add or remove them from the */etc/fstab* file.

Note   Adding entries to the fstab file should ensure the mounts are persisted across reboots. This will not be the case with our systems, as the loop devices created with losetup do not persist the reboot. It is possible to script this with a new systemd unit file to create the loop devices on reboot.

Managing Logical Volumes

Rather than using complete disks or partitions, LVMs or *logical volumes* are often used as an alternative. These are dynamic disks that can easily be extended in ways impossible with physical disks or partitions. We can create a copy of the *partition.yml* Playbook, calling it *lvm.yml* to have Ansible manage logical volumes.

Listing 14-6. Managing Logical Volumes with Ansible Playbooks

```
$ cp partition.yml lvm.yml
$ vim lvm.yml
---
- name: Using LVMs
  hosts: 172.16.120.161
  gather_facts: no
  become: true
  tasks:
    - name: Partition loop0 P2
      parted:
        device: /dev/loop0
        part_start: 50%
        part_end: 100%
        number: 2
        flags: [ lvm ]
        state: present
    - name: Create Volume Group
      lvg:
        vg: vg1
        pvs: /dev/loop0p2
    - name: Create LV
      lvol:
```

```
    lv: lv1
    vg: vg1
    size: 100%FREE
    shrink: false
- name: Create XFS filesystem on lv1
  filesystem:
    dev: /dev/vg1/lv1
    fstype: xfs
- name: Create mount point
  file:
    path: "{{ item }}"
    state: directory
  loop:
    - /data
    - /data/lv1
- name: Mount lv1 to /data/lv1
  mount:
    path: /data/lv1
    src: /dev/vg1/lv1
    fstype: xfs
    state: mounted
```

$ **ansible-playbook lvm.yml**

...

$ **tail -n1 /etc/fstab**

/dev/vg1/lv1 /data/lv1 xfs defaults 0 0

$ **mount -t xfs**

/dev/mapper/cl-root on / type xfs (rw,relatime,seclabel,attr2,i
node64,noquota)

/dev/loop0p1 on /data/p1 type xfs (rw,relatime,seclabel,attr2,i
node64,noquota)

/dev/mapper/vg1-lv1 on /data/lv1 type xfs (rw,relatime,seclabel
,attr2,inode64,noquota)

One side effect of copying the file is thinking we have made all the necessary changes when we haven't. Take care when editing the Playbook to make the required changes; these include the device name and partition number. The edited existing content is highlighted for you in my output. We can see, though, that managing logical volumes is as easy as managing physical devices when combined with the Ansible *lvg* and *lvol* modules. Don't forget with any of these new modules we introduce to research what can be done, using the **ansible-doc lvol** command or whatever module you need help on.

Managing VDO with Ansible

VDO is one of the new features of RHEL 8 but its actual debut was in RHEL 7.5. Using VDO we can create an extra Kernel layer that sits between the block device and the filesystem, allowing for data deduplication and compression.

Updating a Managed Host

We need to make sure that we have both the VDO tools and the Kernel module installed. Installing the VDO Kernel module will ensure that we also have the latest Kernel installed. For this reason, it is best to check that the system is updated and rebooted to ensure we are booted with the correct Kernel. This can be done with Ansible, including the reboot, but as we are working on the controller node, we will drop our own connection to the Ansible engine on the reboot. In order to demonstrate this, we will initially use the CentOS 8 client for the update before we do an update manually on the controller. We will not use this client system for VDO, only the controller. I merely want to demonstrate the update and reboot and some additional Ansible features.

We only want to reboot if the update is needed, so for this we know to use a *handler*. By default, handlers will run **after all tasks**. In a real VDO deployment, we would need to reboot the managed device if a new Kernel was added, ensuring the running Kernel matches the version of the Kernel module. The reboot would need to happen before the Playbook continues by creating the VDO device. We would ideally have a single Playbook that performed the update, reboot, and VDO creation. To ensure that the reboot happens before the remaining VDO tasks, we use the Ansible *meta* module to force the reboot handler at the correct time.

As well as learning about the *meta* module, we want to look at a new way to use variables. We will run a new task to collect the Kernel version after the reboot on the client system. Rather than printing the version directly to the Ansible controllers screen, we can also use the *register* operator to store the output in an array variable. This is great for your learning looking at new options for variable population, as if we haven't seen enough already!

Listing 14-7. Rebooting the Client Device After an Update

```
$ vim update.yml
---
- name: Update and reboot
  hosts: 172.16.120.185
  gather_facts: no
  become: true
  tasks:
    - name: Update all packages
      package:
        name: '*'
        state: latest
      notify: reboot
    - name: run handlers now
      meta: flush_handlers
```

```
  - name: Collect Kernel
    shell: "uname -r"
    register: kernel_version
  - name: Show Kernel
    debug:
      msg: "The kernel is: {{ kernel_version.stdout }}"
handlers:
  - name: reboot
    reboot:
```

$ **ansible-playbook update.yml**
PLAY [Update and reboot]

TASK [Update all packages]
changed: [172.16.120.185]

RUNNING HANDLER [reboot]
changed: [172.16.120.185]

TASK [Collect Kernel]
changed: [172.16.120.185]

TASK [Show Kernel] **
****
ok: [172.16.120.188] => {
    "msg": "The kernel is: 4.18.0-240.1.1.el8_3.x86_64"
}

Note   The variable *kernel_version* is an array storing many elements, not just *stdout*. These include the executed command and start time as examples. If you list the complete variable, you will see the full content. We just need the output, which is retrieved from *kernel_version.stdout*.

The complete Playbook will run. After the reboot we should see the printed Kernel version. Running the Playbook again, we should observe that the reboot does not occur as a handler; it is only executed when the update occurs.

Updating the Controller

Note   With CentOS 8.3 the RAM requirement increases for VDO. If your test system is running with less than 1GB RAM, I would recommend increasing the RAM assigned to the VM to 2GB. If necessary, you can reduce the virtual machines that you have running now, and make do with just the controller node.

To update the controller, we will manually run **yum** and then the reboot. Remember, we are doing this to make sure we have the latest Kernel so when we add Kernel modules, the versions will match. Before we reboot, we may choose to comment the two new lines added to the */etc/fstab* file. The *loop* devices we created will be lost on the reboot. As a quick edit, we choose to use **sed** to delete the last line of the file. We run that command twice, ensuring the two newly added lines are removed. It is a quick edit, but you need to be certain that you do need to remove the last two lines and they are what you expect. Take care on your own systems.

Listing 14-8. Updating the Controller Node and Rebooting

```
$ sudo sed -i '$d' /etc/fstab
$ sudo sed -i '$d' /etc/fstab
$ sudo yum update -y && reboot
```

Working at the command line of the controller, we can update the complete system; we only reboot if the **yum** command succeeds.

Deploying VDO

We will need to create a new raw disk file of at least 5GB for the loop device that we will use as the underlying storage for VDO. VDO required at least 4GB storage, and much of this space is used as a cache drive to allow expansion of compressed files if space is limited on the rest of the drive.

Listing 14-9. Creating Loop Device for VDO

```
$ cd $HOME/ansible/disk
$ fallocate -l 5G disk1
$ sudo losetup /dev/loop1 disk1
```

We can now turn out attention to VDO with Ansible. VDO is an objective of the RHCSA for RHEL 8 and we don't cover it in detail here. This is enough to install VDO, and create and mount VDO devices. This is run only on the controller node.

Listing 14-10. Managing VDO with Ansible

```
$ vim vdo.yml
---
- name: Managing VDO in Ansible
  hosts: 172.16.120.161
  become: true
  gather_facts: false
  tasks:
    - name: Install VDO
      package:
        name:
          - vdo
          - kmod-kvdo
        state: latest
    - name: Start VDO service
```

```
      service:
        name: vdo
        enabled: true
        state: started
    - name: Create VDO device
      vdo:
        name: vdo1
        state: present
        device: /dev/loop1
        logicalsize: 10G
    - name: Format VDO device
      filesystem:
        type: xfs
        dev: /dev/mapper/vdo1
    - name: Create Mount Point
      file:
        path: "{{ item }}"
        state: directory
      loop:
        - /data
        - /data/vdo
    - name: Mount VDO filesystem
      mount:
        path: /data/vdo
        fstype: xfs
        state: mounted
        src: /dev/mapper/vdo1
        opts: defaults,x-systemd.requires=vdo.service
$ ansible-playbook vdo.yml

PLAY [Managing VDO in Ansible]
```

```
TASK [Install VDO]
ok: [172.16.120.161]

TASK [Start VDO service]
ok: [172.16.120.161]

TASK [Create VDO device]
changed: [172.16.120.161]

TASK [Format VDO device]
changed: [172.16.120.161]

TASK [Create Mount Point]
ok: [172.16.120.161] => (item=/data)
changed: [172.16.120.161] => (item=/data/vdo)

TASK [Mount VDO filesystem]
changed: [172.16.120.161]

PLAY RECAP
172.16.120.161                  : ok=6    changed=6    unreachable=0
    failed=0    skipped=0    rescued=0    ignored=0
```

You now have created a VDO device and mounted it to its own directory. Files added to this directory will be automatically compressed if space will be gained. For example, adding JPEG images that are already compressed will not benefit from additional compression, whereas text log files that are archived here will benefit from compression. If you are storing virtual machine images or containers in this directory, each block is examined to see if it's duplicated elsewhere on the VDO device; if it is, there is no need to duplicate that block. These are common features of storage devices these days, and it is nice to see it as a filesystem agnostic feature of CentOS versions > 7.5.

Archiving Files

While we are looking at filesystems, we may as well look at backing up files and directories using the Ansible *archive* module. The default format for the created files is to use the *gzip* compression algorithm, but other formats can be used. If you want to create a *tgz* archive, you must specify a directory as the source. We may want to use this to create an archive of the Apache DocumentRoot on each host.

Listing 14-11. Archiving Directories

```
$ cd $HOME/ansible/disk
$ vim archive.yml
---
- name: Backup web
  hosts: all
  become: true
  gather_facts: false
  tasks:
    - name: Archive DocRoot
      archive:
        path: /var/www/html/
        dest: /root/web.tgz
        format: gz
$ ansible-playbook archive.yml
$ ansible all -b -m command -a "tar -tzf /root/web.tgz
warn=false"
  172.16.120.188 | CHANGED | rc=0 >>
    contact.html
    server.html
    test.php
    index.html
```

```
172.16.120.185 | CHANGED | rc=0 >>
  index.html
  contact.html
  server.html
  test.php
172.16.120.161 | CHANGED | rc=0 >>
  index.html
  contact.html
  server.html
  test.php
```

The Playbook creates the archive on each host and we can use the *ad hoc* command to list the contents of the archive. We turn off warnings in this case; if we don't, Ansible advises us that we could make use of the *unarchive* module instead of the **tar** command. We only want to list the contents, which is why the command is good.

Maintenance of Filesystems

Our last objective that we look at in this chapter is *parallelism* of tasks in Ansible. Consider how many systems tasks should run on in parallel with each other. The more resources we have on the controller node, the more systems we could manage at the same time. The default number of forks is set to 5; as we have only 3 managed nodes, this has not been a problem for us. If we were managing 50 hosts, this relatively low value may impact on the speed of the Playbook execution.

Listing 14-12. The Default Forks Are Set to 5

```
$ ansible-config dump | grep -i fork
DEFAULT_FORKS(default) = 5
```

Setting **forks=20** within the *[defaults]* header of the ansible.cfg would raise the number of nodes that could be managed at a single time. As well as controlling this setting globally in the *ansible.cfg*, we may want to control this for tasks within a play, for example, if we needed to perform some maintenance of a filesystem. One reason could be because we want to secure the filesystems mount point. This would be three tasks:

- Unmount filesystem

- Change the mode on the mount point

- Remount the filesystem

We should make sure that the mount point directory is secured before the filesystem is mounted. The unmounted directory should only be accessible to the root user. When the directory is mounted, the permissions from the root of the mounted filesystem replace those of the unmounted directory. In this way we prevent users from storing files in the directory when it is not mounted.

We will observe the default behavior that each task runs on the three hosts before moving to the next task. This would mean the three hosts would be simultaneously unavailable, even if only for a few seconds. We can configure the play to ensure that the complete play runs on just one node before progressing to the next node, allowing only one node's filesystem to be unavailable at any one time. We will test this with a simple debug message, first using the defaults and then adjusting the *serial* value in the play.

Listing 14-13. By Default, Each Task Is Executed on Each Node Before Moving On

```
$ cd $HOME/ansible/disk
$ vim serial.yml
---
- name: Serial demo
```

```
  hosts: all
  become: false
  gather_facts: false
  tasks:
    - name: task1
      debug:
        msg: "output1"
    - name: task2
      debug:
        msg: "output2"
$ ansible-playbook serial.yml

PLAY [Serial demo]
TASK [task1]
ok: [172.16.120.161] => {
    "msg": "output1"
}
ok: [172.16.120.185] => {
    "msg": "output1"
}
ok: [172.16.120.188] => {
    "msg": "output1"
}

TASK [task2] ok: [172.16.120.185] => {
    "msg": "output2"
}
ok: [172.16.120.161] => {
    "msg": "output2"
}
ok: [172.16.120.188] => {
    "msg": "output2"
}
```

Using the default settings, we can see that the first task runs on all nodes before the second task is executed on all nodes. If it is important that tasks in the play all run on each node before moving on to the next, we can modify the Playbook.

Listing 14-14. Ensuring All Tasks Complete on a Node Before Progressing to the Next Node

```
$ cd $HOME/ansible/disk
$ vim serial.yml
---
- name: Serial demo
  hosts: all
  become: false
  gather_facts: false
  serial: 1
  tasks:
    - name: task1
      debug:
        msg: "output1"
    - name: task2
      debug:
        msg: "output2"$ ansible-playbook serial.yml
PLAY [Serial demo]
TASK [task1]
ok: [172.16.120.161] => {
    "msg": "output1"
}

TASK [task2]
ok: [172.16.120.161] => {
    "msg": "output2"
}
```

```
PLAY [Serial demo]
TASK [task1]
ok: [172.16.120.185] => {
    "msg": "output1"
}

TASK [task2]
ok: [172.16.120.185] => {
    "msg": "output2"
}

PLAY [Serial demo]

TASK [task1]
ok: [172.16.120.188] => {
    "msg": "output1"
}

TASK [task2]
ok: [172.16.120.188] => {
    "msg": "output2"
}
```

We can see the play listed three times now instead of once. The play is executed on one node at a time with the **serial: 1** setting. This could be a higher value or a percentage value if they were appropriate.

Summary

Ansible is a full-featured configuration management system. Although we have looked mainly at a LAMP deployment in the book so far, there are many more elements of Linux that we can manage. Of course, outside of Linux there are more pastures to investigate. Although only looking at Linux in this course, we can expand to investigate storage, and this is what this chapter was dedicated to.

In trekking through Linux storage with Ansible, we discovered many new Ansible modules. These included:

- *parted*: Partition disks

- *filesystem*: Create filesystems on devices

- *file*: We have used the file module before, but where we could see the state of directory.

- *mount*: Mount filesystems and write to */etc/fstab*

- *lvg*: Manage volume groups in LVM

- *lvol*: Manage Volumes in LVM

- *vdo*: Create VDO devices

- *meta*: Manage Ansible meta information. We used it to force handlers to run ahead of remaining tasks.

- *archive*: Backup files and directories

Not only did we look at storage, we could see the use of the register operator to store output of a task in a variable for later use. We also reminded ourselves of the order in which handlers run, after all tasks. Where we need a reboot to happen before other tasks, we can use the *meta* Ansible module and *flush_handlers* as a task directly after the reboot task. In this way the complete Playbook can run, but tasks that require the reboot can wait for the device reboot before completing.

We finished up looking at how we can control the amount of nodes managed at any one time. We may need to increase this default value of five nodes when we want faster performance or, as we did, by decreasing the serialization so that the complete play executes on one node at a time to suit availability needs.

CHAPTER 15

Managing Scheduled Tasks with Ansible

In this last chapter of the RHCE Study Guide, we concentrate on the final small exam objectives where you need to know how to create and manage scheduled tasks with Ansible in Linux. This may be with either *atd* or *crond*, where *atd* is great for scheduling *ad hoc* Linux commands and *crond* for scheduling jobs that need to be run on a regular interval. For simplicity you can target just your Ansible controller, but we will target all hosts and include both CentOS and Ubuntu in the examples.

Ad Hoc Linux Jobs with ATD

The *at* daemon (atd) allows you to schedule jobs in Linux that need to run at irregular intervals, perhaps even just once, such as when you need to schedule the migration of data between servers over a holiday period.

With a minimal install of CentOS 8 and Ubuntu 18.04, the service is not installed. We will, of course, add this and ensure that it is running before creating jobs. It would be worthwhile creating a role to install and configure the *atd* so we can reference this from any Playbook needing to create a scheduled *at* job.

© Andrew Mallett 2021
A. Mallett, *Red Hat Certified Engineer (RHCE) Study Guide*,
https://doi.org/10.1007/978-1-4842-6861-2_15

Creating the Ansible Role to Manage ATD

We should be experts at creating roles now with **ansible-galaxy**, and this also works as a great memory-jogger.

Listing 15-1. Creating the ATD Role

```
$ ansible-galaxy role init /home/tux/.ansible/roles/atd
- Role $HOME/.ansible/roles/atd was created successfully
$ vim $HOME/.ansible/roles/atd/tasks/main.yml
---
- name: Install AT
  package:
    name: at
    state: present
- name: Manage ATD
  service:
    name: atd
    enabled: true
    state: started
```

Playbook to Create Jobs in At

The role for *atd* is made simple, as the package and service names are consistent across our distributions. It is still well worth creating the role, as potentially we may need to create several different Playbooks needing to schedule *at* jobs. The role means that we can make use of the one lump of code in each required Playbook. The RHCSA covers the creation of scheduled tasks with *at* in more detail, but suffice it to say *at* is used to schedule jobs that may only need to run once rather than regularly. We can schedule jobs using a full date and time or with abbreviations such as Tuesday for next Tuesday. We don't have quite as much flexibility within

Ansible, and we are limited to a count of units. We specify that the job should run based on the count of the specified units. If we wanted a job to run tomorrow, we would specify **count: 1** and **units: days**.

Listing 15-2. Creating at Jobs with Ansible

```
$ mkdir $HOME/ansible/at ; cd $HOME/ansible/at
$ vim at.yml
---
- name: Create at job
  hosts: all
  become: true
  gather_facts: false
  roles:
    - atd
  tasks:
    - name: backup users database tomorrow
      at:
        command: 'tar -czf /root/users.tgz /etc/passwd
                  /etc/group /etc/shadow'
        count: 1
        units: days
        unique: true
$ ansible-playbook at.yml
$ sudo atq
Mon Dec 14 11:53:00 2020 a root
```

Enabling the uniqueness of this job will ensure that we only have the listing for this job once in the job database for *at*. If this was not set, the job would be created on each execution of the Playbook.

Creating Regular Jobs with Cron

Scheduling regular jobs using *cron* is very common in Linux, and the service and tools are installed by default. If we need to create a regular backup of those same files rather than a single backup, we could use *cron*. The following Playbook will create the named file within the */etc/cron.d/* directory and will run at 5.30 AM Monday through Friday.

Listing 15-3. Creating cron Entries with Ansible

```
$ mkdir $HOME/ansible/cron ; cd $HOME/ansible/cron
$ vim cron.yml
---
- name: Manage Cron Entries
  hosts: all
  gather_facts: false
  become: true
  tasks:
    - name: Backup user database
      cron:
        name: Backup Users
        hour: 5
        minute: 30
        weekday: 1-5
        user: root
        job: 'tar -czf /root/user.tgz /etc/passwd /etc/shadow'
        cron_file: user_backup
$ ansible-playbook cron.yml
$ cat /etc/cron.d/user_backup
#Ansible: Backup Users
30 5 * * 1-5 root tar -czf /root/user.tgz /etc/passwd /etc/
shadow
```

As you can see, the demonstration finished by listing the newly created entry in */etc/cron.d*. The name we assign to the *cron job* shows as a comment in the file, making it easily identifiable to ourselves and Ansible.

Summary

You are at the start of the rest of your DevOps or System Administration career. You have journeyed a long way from the start of this book, and you are now ready to commit to your own success. It is you who hold the keys to your own future. In this closing chapter we were able to tidy up some of the loose ends of the exam objectives in looking at scheduled tasks. You learned how to use the *at* module in Ansible for irregular jobs and the *cron* Ansible module where you need those jobs to execute regularly.

You should now ensure that you practice the examples that we have shown in the chapter; as always, it is the effort that you expend that determines your success. I would also recommend reviewing each chapter and seeing how many of the demonstrations you can complete without reference to the complete step-by-step instructions. Good luck and thank you.

Index

A, B

Ad hoc commands
  definition, 47
  inventory groups
    account information, 55
    configuration, 58–59
    $HOME/inventory file, 53
    password, 56
    SSH key-authentication, 57–58
    user account, 55
    variables, 54
  modules, 59–60
  testing
    advantages, 51
    command options, 52
    hosts, 50
    modification, 51
    overwriting option, 50
    ping module, 48
    ping module, 49
Ansible, *see* Red Hat
at daemon (atd)
  cron, 220–221
  playbooks, 218–219
  role creation, 218
  scheduling jobs, 217

C

Configuration file, 11
  ansible.cfg, 14
  current directory, 15
  declare command, 17
  effective configuration, 13–14
  fallback location, 12
  home directory, 14, 23–26
  printing process
    default option, 19
    documentation, 22
    effective settings, 21
    headers cataloging, 20
    regular expressions, 20
    sub-commands, 18
  test security issue, 15
  variables, 16
  working directory/shell
    variables, 12, 18
Copy module
  content argument,
    113, 115–116
  fold operator, 116
  MOTD file, 115
  src argument/sudoers
    files, 114–115

© Andrew Mallett 2021
A. Mallett, *Red Hat Certified Engineer (RHCE) Study Guide*,
https://doi.org/10.1007/978-1-4842-6861-2